The End of Everything: Postmodernism and the Vanishing of the Human

**Lyotard • Haraway • Plato • Heidegger
Habermas • McLuhan**

Foreword by Will Self
Introduction by Stuart Sim
Edited by Richard Appignanesi

ICON BOOKS UK   TOTEM BOOKS USA

Published in the UK in 2003
by Icon Books Ltd., Grange Road,
Duxford, Cambridge CB2 4QF
e-mail: info@iconbooks.co.uk
www.iconbooks.co.uk

Published in the USA in 2003
by Totem Books
Inquiries to: Icon Books Ltd.,
Grange Road, Duxford,
Cambridge CB2 4QF, UK

Sold in the UK, Europe, South Africa
and Asia by Faber and Faber Ltd.,
3 Queen Square, London WC1N 3AU
or their agents

Distributed to the trade in the USA by
National Book Network Inc.,
4720 Boston Way, Lanham,
Maryland 20706

Distributed in the UK, Europe,
South Africa and Asia by
Macmillan Distribution Ltd.,
Houndmills, Basingstoke RG21 6XS

Distributed in Canada by
Penguin Books Canada,
10 Alcorn Avenue, Suite 300,
Toronto, Ontario M4V 3B2

Published in Australia in 2003
by Allen & Unwin Pty. Ltd.,
PO Box 8500, 83 Alexander Street,
Crows Nest, NSW 2065

ISBN 1 84046 421 6

Typesetting by Wayzgoose

Printed and bound in the UK by
Cox & Wyman Ltd., Reading

Contents

Contributors

Richard Appignanesi is Editorial Director of Icon Books and the author of *Introducing Freud* (1999), *Introducing Postmodernism* (1999) and *Introducing Existentialism* (2001), all published by Icon/Totem. He is also the author of *Yukio Mishima's Report to the Emperor* (Sinclair-Stevenson, 2002).

Christopher Horrocks is Senior Lecturer in the faculty of Design at Kingston University. His previous books for Icon/Totem include *Introducing Baudrillard* (1999), *Introducing Foucault* (1999) and *Baudrillard and the Millennium* (1999).

George Myerson writes on contemporary culture and modern thought. He is Reader in English at King's College London, and is also the author of *Ecology and the End of Postmodernity* (Icon/Totem, 2001).

Kieron O'Hara is a senior research fellow in the Intelligence, Agents and Multimedia Group at the University of Southampton. He co-wrote the script of the computer game *Tomb Raider 4*, and is the author of the forthcoming *Trust: A Popular History* (Icon, 2004).

Will Self is an acclaimed author, journalist and critic. His novels include *My Idea of Fun* (Bloomsbury, 1993), *Great Apes* (Penguin, 1998), *How the Dead Live* (Bloomsbury, 2000) and *Dorian* (Viking, 2002). He has also published a number of collections of short stories and two books of collected journalism and criticism.

Stuart Sim is Professor of Critical Theory in the Department of English at the University of Sunderland. His most recent books are *Contemporary Continental Philosophy: The New Scepticism* (Ashgate, 2000), *Post-Marxism: An Intellectual History* (Routledge, 2000) and *Irony and Crisis: A Critical History of Postmodern Culture* (Icon/Totem, 2002).

Foreword

Will Self

If, as Mallarmé said, 'Beliefs are ideas going bald', then ours is an age in which a myriad of trichologically challenged men and women are fighting to the death over a single broken, pink, plastic comb. In the chance meeting between an umbrella and a sewing machine, which takes place on the dissecting table of the television screen every minute of every hour of every day of every week of every year, no new devices are spontaneously engineered. Rather, the *sine qua non* of the postmodern *Weltanschauung* has been revealed – especially in the past two years – to be a cut-and-paste job on the human condition. The failure of the Millennium itself to provide anything much beyond some achingly dull television retrospectives has set the leaden seal on a period of uncompromising creative entropy.

The erection of the terrorist detumescers of the American phallocracy as some retro-standard of Belief does not – in and of itself – provide the West with a new idea, any more than taking the contrary view – www.alQaeda.com – will lead us into an ideological Eden. Only history will record whether the new Islamic fundamentalisms (and they are multifarious) will turn out to be – in the *badinage* of the locker room – 'growers or showers'.

The five essays gathered together in this volume are a collective cautionary tale about how a catch-all for an architectural style became a synonym for intellectual alopecia. Communication, genetic modification, virtuality, 'inhumanism', the so-called 'knowledge economy' – all of them, a filigree of fine hairs moulting onto coarse Neanderthal shoulders. By thrusting Heidegger, Habermas, McLuhan, Lyotard, Haraway *et al* down into the padded chair, and subjecting them to a brutal electronic shearing with the number one clippers, Myerson, Horrocks and

Sim show a peculiar courage. The tonsure of postmodernism is obliged to confront itself gleaming in the plate glass mirror, while these bold barbers enquire: 'Something for the weekend, sir?'

Only Plato rises from the chair, his flowing locks shampooed, conditioned and waved. Only Plato can afford to pay for hairdressing rather than barbering. Only Plato has a hot date – a threesome with Futurity and Posterity. It's a tribute to their freedom from cant, and their willingness to go scrumping in the groves of academe, that these writers avoid either bowdlerising or catechising. It's a sad fact about the landscape of postmodernism that so much is a mirage of a mirage, a complex set of interactions between convection (hot air) and reflection (unoriginality) resulting in the superimposition of one illusion upon another.

All the best postmodern encounters should be in dark alleys, fetish clubs, small presses. The protagonists shouldn't be obliged to place tendentious advertisements in the impersonal columns of newspapers: Smooth Ariel seeks Hairy Caliban, with a view to mutual transplantation fun. GSOH essential. From the viewpoint of our children and our children's children, the heady time when there was hair to spare – so much that we could fashion dreadlocks, Afros and perms; shape it, dye it, spike it – will be both incredible and worthy of contempt. How they will tire of us telling them about the decades when there were still ideas and not merely beliefs. So, in order to preserve us from their studied – and fanatical – contempt, how convenient it will be for us to have this volume handy, with which to parry their blows.

Introduction

Stuart Sim

The French cultural theorist Michel Foucault once remarked that he could imagine a future in which 'man would be erased, like a face drawn in sand at the edge of the sea'.[1] It was a particular concept of 'man' that he had in mind rather than humanity itself, but Foucault's prophecy might well come true in a more radical sense than he intended. There are forces within our culture that could lead to humanity as we know it becoming irrelevant, or perhaps even vanishing altogether. What those forces are is what this volume is concerned to explore – and it is technology that goes into the dock for cross-examination.

It is one of the paradoxes of modernity that a socio-cultural movement which sought to liberate the individual – from material want, religious superstition and arbitrary political power in the first instance – has also paved the way for a new form of domination that many find even more insidious: the domination of humanity by technology. While it has to be acknowledged that technology has played a major role in enabling us to create a new kind of society, one less in thrall to tradition than, say, European feudal society, it also has its more sinister side. Technology, or 'techno-science' as cultural commentators now tend to refer to it, can, and does, take on a dynamic of its own. It is a dynamic that in its more extreme forms can reduce humanity to the status of slaves serving the machine (reversing the traditional notion of the relationship), and even threaten the existence of human life itself. Developments in techno-science – in Artificial Intelligence and Artificial Life most notably – suggest that eventually the human could be eclipsed. As the feminist theorist, and champion of the cyborg concept, Donna Haraway so memorably put it, 'the machine is us':[2] a conclusion calculated to alienate more of 'us',

1

one suspects, than it will attract. The benefits of a union between the human and the non-human are by no means as self-evident as Haraway assumes. Somehow one cannot envisage this as a reciprocal relationship either, or that machines are about to communicate back – however they might manage it – with the message that 'the human is us'. Instead, the fear would be that the more it becomes the case that 'the machine is us', then the likelier is the possibility of the human simply withering away. Immersed in the new technology though it may be, that is an outcome that postmodernism as a movement has set itself to resist. The end of the human is to such thinkers the end of everything that really matters.

Technology as simultaneously liberation and threat is the issue addressed in all the essays in this volume, which collectively scrutinise the complex response we have to the onward march of techno-science in a postmodern world in which the old cultural certainties have, for better or worse, lapsed. We tend to divide our world up into the 'natural' and the 'non-natural', but as George Myerson points out in 'Donna Haraway and GM Foods', that is to make assumptions about the purity of entities, such as both humans and what they eat, that will not necessarily stand up to very close inspection. Haraway is in favour of the boundary transgressions involved in genetic engineering, while sensitive to the dangers of such experiments being under the control of multinational corporations, or 'hypercapitalism'. In this new culture the cyborg becomes the norm – whether a cyborg-human or a cyborg-fruit such as the 'Flavr Savr' tomato with its added gene taken from, unlikely as it may seem, the deep-sea flounder. Like it or not, Myerson notes, we have now entered a world that will be defined by an ambiguity regarding species, rather than the clear-cut category divisions by which we have tended to operate in the past. Not so much the end of everything, as the beginning of an era of constantly changing things that sometimes offer liberation, sometimes threat. Whether we can always distinguish one from the other is another question, and the dilemma posed by the cyborg forms one of the recurring motifs of our essays.

The end of everything was a topic that obsessed the philosopher Jean-François Lyotard towards the end of his life, as we learn in my own essay 'Lyotard and the Inhuman'. Lyotard foresaw a world in which the combined forces of techno-science would devote all their resources to maintaining life past the predicted 'heat death' of our sun. Only it would not be human life that survived the event, but computer life – that is, Artificial Intelligence/Artificial Life, or, as Lyotard perceived it, the 'inhuman'. In effect, techno-science would continue the project of modernity, stripping it down to its most basic element, the development of ever-greater levels of operational efficiency, in order to ensure the survival of the system. Loyalty to the system is the watchword of the techno-scientific project. In such a process, humans are an impediment to success, being too inefficient, too independent-minded, ultimately just too unreliable. To disrupt the progress of the grand narrative of techno-science was for Lyotard, therefore, to preserve the human. The machines were not to be allowed to win; not without a fight anyway.

Arguably the farthest-reaching changes brought about by the new technology have come in the field of communication. The Internet, the World Wide Web, e-mail and the mobile phone have transformed the character of communication within a generation, and, many would also claim, the character of the communicators themselves. George Myerson considers these dramatic changes in 'Heidegger, Habermas and the Mobile Phone', speculating that the humble mobile phone might turn out to be the most revolutionary of all the new technologies, since it can function as our personal entry point into all those other systems. A famous advertisement of the 1960s told us that 'you're never alone with a Strand [cigarette]'; the twenty-first century equivalent would have to be that 'you're never alone with a mobile phone', with its offer of instant access to a host of communication systems no matter where you happen to be

('I'm on the train ...'). Again, there is a sense in which the technology can be regarded as both an empowering and a disempowering force. The easier it is to communicate, the more we become divorced from meaningful human contact. 'M-communication', paradoxically enough for something that offers us so many personal options, might end up robbing us of our individuality: 'The mobile would be the supreme medium for turning everything around into a system, driving out the process of reaching understanding, replacing meaning with messages, consensus with instructions and insight with information.' The models of communication put forward by Heidegger and Habermas, with their emphasis precisely on meaning, understanding, consensus and insight, provide us with correctives to the dehumanising tendencies implicit in m-communication.

What the Internet constitutes for Kieron O'Hara is a full-scale challenge to our existing conceptions of the nature, and social role, of knowledge. In 'Plato and the Internet' he argues that old theories of knowledge – that is, epistemologies (ranging back to the seminal work of Plato on the subject) – have been made redundant by the new technology. Forget 'justified true belief' (justified by philosophical methods); 'know-how', an entity largely ignored by epistemologists throughout philosophical history, is the new currency, and this calls for a fundamental change in the way we conceive of knowledge. In O'Hara's model of epistemology, know-how, or 'procedural knowledge', is the key element. Procedural knowledge provides us with the means to overcome information overload, one of the critical problems generated by the Internet, as all regular users are only too painfully aware. Knowledge in the Internet age is to be characterised as 'usable information', and knowing how to use it is the most prized skill – and possibly the way of holding on to our humanity when confronted by the inhuman scale of the Internet system. Traditional epistemology, O'Hara contends, has no role to play in the new knowledge economy; indeed, for him it is as outmoded as alchemy.

4

The most famous theorist of the new media in the twentieth century was undoubtedly Marshall McLuhan, whose observation that 'the medium is the message' has long since passed into the popular consciousness. McLuhan's legacy is investigated by Christopher Horrocks in 'Marshall McLuhan and Virtuality'. The development of new technologies such as the Internet has, Horrocks notes, spurred a revival of interest in McLuhan's work, which rapidly went out of fashion after his death in 1980. McLuhan is often presented now as a prophet of the new technologies, in which increasingly the medium does seem to be the message (think of virtual reality systems, for example); but Horrocks is careful to bring out his critical side too. In common with many postmodernist theorists, McLuhan recognised that technology had as much of a capacity to enslave us as to liberate us. Horrocks feels that McLuhan's theories 'can provide the means to temper more strident versions of cyborg theory', pointing out that his subject is suspicious of any media that 'weaken' the individual's 'sense of having a physical body and an autonomous identity'. The cyborg announces the eclipse of the human for yet another commentator.

Postmodernism has an ambivalent attitude towards technology, therefore, and it seems likely that it will continue to be very wary of the machinations of techno-science. If there is a spectre haunting our culture now, it is the spectre of the techno-scientific system itself, which regards the human as, at best, a hindrance to the maintaining of its operational efficiency. It could be argued that monitoring that system, in all its diversity and complexity, is the major task of the cultural commentator in a postmodern world. The five essays included in this volume are thought-provoking contributions to that monitoring process, all concerned with ensuring that the human is not allowed to vanish in the face of accelerated technological advance – a 'Campaign for Real Humanity', we could say.

Notes

1. Michel Foucault, *The Order of Things: An Archaeology of the Human Sciences*, trans. A.M. Sheridan Smith (London: Tavistock, 1970), p. 387.
2. Donna Haraway, *Simians, Cyborgs, and Women: The Reinvention of Nature* (New York: Routledge, 1991), p. 180.

Lyotard and the Inhuman

Stuart Sim

The Death of the Universe

We live in a universe with an expiry date. Between 4.5 billion and 6 billion years from now (estimates vary, but 6 billion appears to be the upper limit), the sun will have suffered a 'heat death' and life on earth will be over. Dramatic (and even melo-dramatic) though this may sound on first hearing, in the early twenty-first century few of us are likely to lose too much sleep over such a projected scenario, given a time-span that is all but unimaginable to us as individuals surviving for only a few decades each. There seems little sense of urgency about such a prospect from where we now stand, and, for the time being at any rate, life goes on as normal.

One recent exception to such apathy about the ultimate fate of the universe, however, was the philosopher Jean-François Lyotard, who towards the end of his life (he died in 1998) became somewhat obsessed with the topic, speculating in *The Inhuman* (1988) as to what the projected death of the sun might mean for the condition of humankind now.[1] 'The human race is already in the grip of the necessity of having to evacuate the solar system in 4.5 billion years', he informed us, attempting to inject a note of urgency into the debate.[2]

Lyotard is best known for the positive message of *The Postmodern Condition* (1979), an enquiry into the status of knowledge in late twentieth-century culture, which announced the decline of oppressive 'grand narratives' – in effect, ideologies – and the rise of a new cultural paradigm based on scepticism towards universal explanatory theories in general.[3] According to Lyotard, humanity now had the opportunity to pursue a myriad of 'little narratives' instead, returning political power to the individual and threatening the power base of the authoritarian state (and states in general are authoritarian to the postmodern-ist thinker). The postmodern era he pictured promised to be one of liberation from ideological servitude. In *The Inhuman*, less than a decade later, a much darker tone prevails that suggests humanity has acquired a new set of enemies to replace the grand narratives of yesteryear.

We shall consider Lyotard's argument in *The Inhuman* in more detail at a later point – suffice it to say for the present he expresses the fear that computers eventually will be programmed to take over from human beings, with the goal of prolonging 'life' past the point of the heat death of the sun. It will not, however, be *human* life that survives, and Lyotard is deeply opposed to any shift towards such an 'inhuman' solution, which, he claims, has the backing of the forces of 'techno-science' (technology plus science plus advanced capitalism, the multinationals and so on).

Lyotard's response is to call for a campaign against techno-science and all its works: 'What else remains as "politics" except resistance to the inhuman?', as he puts it, inviting us to join him in opposition against the planned eclipse of the human by advanced technology.[4] His task as a writer and philosopher, as he sees it, is to ensure that we 'bear witness' to such a process, so that techno-science does not succeed in imposing its programme on us by stealth – an outcome that, given the power and prestige enjoyed by techno-science in our society, is only too likely.[5] The feminist theorist Donna Haraway's remark that science is 'the real game in town, the one we must play', captures the general perception well.[6]

Lyotard's reflections have a wider significance than the particular problem he is addressing, and these do merit closer attention. Whether we are aware of it or not, the inhuman has infiltrated our daily existence to a quite remarkable degree – in the sense of the supersession of the human by the technological. For the remainder of this study, we will consider a range of arguments on the topic of the inhuman, running from critics such as Lyotard to enthusiasts such as the feminist theorists Donna Haraway and Sadie Plant, taking excursions into medical technology, computer technology, computer viruses, Artificial Intelligence (AI), Artificial Life (AL), humanism and, finally, science-fictional narrative (William Gibson) along the way (see 'Key Ideas' at the end of this essay).

The infiltration of the inhuman into our everyday concerns demands such a wide range of reference. After engaging with the arguments, we may decide it is more appropriate to fear, resist, welcome, actively encourage or perhaps just simply tolerate the inhuman; but one thing is certain – we cannot avoid it.

Living with the Inhuman

To speak of infiltration is to be emotive, but it can be defended. The inhuman is now with us in a variety of forms, and technology is encroaching ever further into our lives – even to the extent of breaching the boundaries of our physical bodies on occasion. Bionic man (or woman) is no longer the fanciful notion it may once have seemed as the basis for various screen narratives or comic-book tales.

Medical science has long since introduced the inhuman into the human (think of heart pacemakers, to take an uncontroversial, and widely used, example of the conjunction of man and machine, or kidney dialysis machines), and that is a trend that can only intensify as medical technology becomes all the more sophisticated. Then there are life-support machines (in reality a complex of machines collectively taking over key bodily functions when these lapse). At least in theory, these could keep us 'alive' for decades after what in earlier times would have been classified as death pure and simple. Whether someone whose vital functions would cease without such mechanical help is actually 'alive' in the normal understanding of the term has proved to be an interesting question with many ramifications – moral and legal, for example – that are still avidly being explored by doctors, lawyers and philosophers alike.

Add to this that computers now run vast areas of Western social existence, from home-heating systems through to airline flights and nuclear power stations, reducing the human dimension to the point where we can seem irrelevant to the operation of such systems.

The vexed question of AI has to be confronted in such cases, given there are computer systems that no longer have any need of human input, being self-sustaining – and even, in their own particular way, capable of reproduction. Computer viruses, for example, have the ability to transform themselves in a bewildering variety of ways that certainly hint at both intelligence and reproductive capacity.

When Lyotard rails against techno-science, it is really AI that he is targeting: that is the area where the main problems lie for defenders of the human. AI raises the spectre of another advanced life-form contesting our domination of the planet and its resources – at which point the nature of the inhuman becomes, in every sense of the word, very much a 'live' issue for all of us. No one could be impartial if such a conflict came to pass. Living with the inhuman, as we do now, is one thing; being subordinated to its will would be quite something else.

The Death of Humanism?

Humanism may be seen as one of those phenomena that, like motherhood and world peace, no one could possibly raise substantial objections to – or if they did, only for the purposes of being thought iconoclastic. How could one not be in favour of furthering the cause of the human race, and, in particular, providing a context for individual self-expression and self-realisation? Yet if poststructuralism and postmodernism are to be believed, we now live in a post-humanist world.

None of the major theorists in those movements – iconoclasts to a person, it should be noted – has much good to say of humanism, which is identified in their minds with modernity and hence held to be responsible for most of our current cultural ills. For such thinkers, humanism equals the 'Enlightenment project', with its cult of reason and belief in perpetual material progress, and, as such, is something to be rejected in our much more circumspect, postmodern, culture. Pessimism has now established a strong hold on the postmodern mind, to replace the unbounded optimism associated with the modern, and human limitations are more readily acknowledged than in the recent cultural past. Reason alone is no longer seen to be our eternal saviour.

Humanism is also taken to equal advanced capitalism, political repression, the destruction of most of the planet's renewable resources, and grand narratives – Marxism, liberal democracy or capitalism, for example – that demand our submission to their will. For some, it also equals the mental set that sanctioned events such as the Holocaust, where domination over one's environment, and desire for 'rational solutions' to perceived social 'problems', were taken to logical and horrific conclusions. The philosopher Theodor Adorno, an important influence on the poststructuralist and postmodernist movements, is famed for his remark that '[t]o write poetry after Auschwitz is barbaric' – the point being that we could only be appalled at where the exercise of reason had led us in this instance.[7]

Post-humanism takes its lead from sentiments like this. Lyotard regards such 'rationality' as endemic to capitalism, which he conceives as a 'monad' – meaning it is a self-contained entity oblivious to everything except its own interests. 'When the point is to extend the capacities of the monad', he claims, 'it seems reasonable to abandon, or even actively to destroy, those parts of the human race which appear superfluous, useless for that goal. For example, the populations of the Third World.'[8]

While humanism may have started as a movement to liberate humankind from the dead weight of tradition, it has declined into a tradition itself, so the story goes, oppressing humankind in its turn. It is therefore to be resisted and undermined wherever possible. As far as poststructuralism and postmodernism are concerned, humanism is dead – and good riddance too, seems to be the general reaction. Time to reassess where we are going culturally: 'Why do we have to save money and time to the point where this imperative seems like the law of our lives?', Lyotard demands, dramatising the point that we have internalised the dynamics of modernity into our very being, as if that were the only possible way to behave.[9] Modernity and humanism conspire to be a particularly sophisticated form of social brainwashing.

Humanism is so generally reviled in theoretical circles these days that it is all too easy to forget its good points – and it most certainly had these. Its championship of reason constituted a principled challenge to the rule of superstition, and those who exploited superstition for their own ideological ends (organised religion being one outstanding example of that process in action).

The Holocaust is not the only possible outcome for such a programme, as certain thinkers would seem to be implying in their critiques of the humanist legacy. When we criticise the Enlightenment project for its failings, we might just wonder what kind of society we would be living in now had it never taken place. Pre-Enlightenment European society was not exactly kind to the individual, whom it kept in a state of more or less permanent subjection. At the very least, the emphasis on reason enabled some individuals (more and more as time went on) to escape the clutches of arbitrary authority and develop their abilities more than they would otherwise have been allowed to do.

Humanism has its weaknesses, as even its most fervent supporters must concede, but its historical record is not necessarily as bad as it is sometimes made out to be. To reduce it to a 'monad in expansion' is to do it a considerable disservice.[10]

The Rise of Inhumanism

Post-humanism implies a very different attitude towards the individual. This shift of perspective can take many different forms. One possible move is into what we might call 'inhuman-ism': a deliberate blurring of the lines between human beings and machines, going well past the point of current medical procedures.

Inhumanism calls for a reassessment of the significance of the human, and a realignment of our relationship to technology. It is just such a process that Lyotard, for all his post-humanist bias, was so afraid of, and which he was repeatedly warning us against in his late career. The more we consider the point, how-ever, the more we are forced to recognise that inhumanism is now an integral part of our lives. The relationship between human and machine has altered dramatically in recent decades. Where once that relationship was one of domination with humans firmly in control, increasingly it has become one of co-operation – and even sometimes of domination from the machine side (particularly so when it comes to the more sophisti-cated forms of AI).

How far we are willing to allow the latter phenomenon to continue developing is an interesting moral dilemma – arguably the most important moral dilemma of our age. Haraway might argue that 'the machine is us', and even celebrate this supposed state of affairs, but many will be deeply worried at such a prospect.[11] Thus we find Lyotard wondering, 'What if what is "proper" to humankind were to be inhabited by the inhuman?'[12]

It is a question that goes right to the heart of what it means to be human and our vision of our place in the universal scheme. Locating the boundaries of the 'proper' is an activity with impli-cations for all of the human race, as is the question of whether these boundaries can be, or even should be, policed. Even AI enthusiasts can see problems arising, with Hugo de Garis, look-ing ahead to the creation of super-AI entities called 'artilects', predicting that '[t]he issues of massive intelligence will dominate global politics in the next century'.[13]

It is a dilemma that faces us more and more as technology makes ever greater inroads into our lives. As noted earlier, we live in a culture that is almost totally dependent on computers for the operation of its various systems. Think of the fears that were around in the 1990s over a possible millennium meltdown of the computer system at large (the Y2K – year 2000 – problem), which would have left us almost helpless.

Doomsday scenarios were postulated in the run-up to the event itself: planes falling out of the sky; the collapse of all public utilities, leading to looting and perhaps the breakdown of public order and our political systems; the malfunctioning of nuclear power stations, with catastrophic consequences for the planet's ecology; epidemics that could not be checked – and a host of other such scare stories.

In the event, the worst-case scenario did not occur and we breathed a collective sigh of relief; but no one had any very clear idea as to the best course of action to take if it had (except, as some of the more hysterical voices counselled, to hide away with a cache of tinned food, some bottled water and a gun to protect oneself from looters).

It became apparent from the Y2K situation just how much of our autonomy we had ceded to our computer systems, and that it was more a case of them controlling us than the other way around. Without computers we no longer seemed to have the basis for a properly functioning civil society, and if Y2K has been safely negotiated that does not mean we shall be any the less vulnerable to system breakdown if it ever does occur on a significant scale. In fact, as technology attains new levels of sophistication, we shall most likely become even *more* vulnerable than ever.

Lyotard summed up the dilemma we face in this regard quite neatly when he pointed out one of the lessons we learn from catastrophe theory: 'It is not true that uncertainty (lack of control) decreases as accuracy goes up: it goes up as well.'[14] In other words, the more efficient computers become, the more we rely on their operation for the systems we depend on to run our daily lives, then the more we are at their mercy. Anyone whose computer has ever 'crashed' will know just what this can mean at the local level; magnify this and full-scale social disaster looms.

There is little evidence of any concerted movement away from computer dependence, especially now that Y2K has proved to be a non-problem. And as evidence of just how vulnerable we are becoming, as this essay was being written the so-called 'love bug' virus was creating havoc among the world's e-mail systems. 'It's a very effective virus. It's one of the most aggressive and nastiest I've ever seen. It manifests itself almost everywhere in the computer', said an industry spokesperson of an 'entity' that managed to shut down 10 per cent of the world's e-mail servers within a day, causing billions of dollars of damage as it spread.[15]

Doomsday scenarios are not hard to imagine given such events, and no doubt even nastier and more aggressive viruses are waiting in the wings to appear in due course (perhaps even before this collection of essays is published). The battle for control of cyberspace has already begun in earnest.

Medical technology sets us a host of interesting problems concerning the inhuman. We mentioned heart pacemakers and kidney dialysis machines earlier, but few will see these as posing acute moral dilemmas. Their use is now so widespread that they have become an accepted part of our lives – although how far down that line we can travel while still respecting 'what is "proper" to humankind' is an open question.

Life-support machines will become progressively more successful in replicating the body's systems in years to come – as, no doubt, will the processes involved in keeping premature babies alive at even earlier stages of gestation than at present (23 weeks being the current threshold for likely survival). Artificial organs have already made their appearance and will probably become standard practice before too long (although how effective they may be in the longer term is another issue).

Do we become less than human if key parts of our bodies are not 'natural' tissue? How many synthetic body parts can we tolerate without losing 'what is "proper" to humankind' in the process? Will consciousness, for example, be affected by a body containing significant amounts of non-natural tissue (perhaps even inside the brain), or dependent on computer regulation for its normal functioning? No one really knows the answers to such questions as yet, but the problem is already looming large on the horizon and will have to be confronted eventually.

Possibly the most contentious area in inhumanism is AI, which many scientists regard as constituting a recognisable life-form in its own right. AI may need human input initially, but once under way it can, and does, take on an existence of its own, apparently independent of human concerns and with its own internal dynamic. As a case in point, the 'love bug' virus very soon started to mutate into more complex formulations that rendered it all the more difficult to track down and neutralise. Complexity theory would suggest that at a certain level of development, AI systems (like most 'natural' systems) could spontaneously mutate, by means of 'emergent processes', so-called, to higher levels of organisation – perhaps even to consciousness and self-consciousness. At that stage, we are talking about AL, with the existence of viruses reinforcing the notion of alternative life-forms (in the sense of life consisting of a struggle for survival within an often hostile environment). We could then speak of 'what is "proper" to inhumankind', with the interesting prospect, of course, that this may well clash with what is proper to us as humans – or HL (Human Life) as we might style the latter.

The science writer Mark Ward has noted that,

Artificial Life research encompasses software simulations, robotics, protein electronics and even attempts to re-create the Earth's first living organisms. It is less concerned with what something is built of than with how it lives. It is concerned with dynamics and just how life keeps going.[16]

AL may well have completely different imperatives to HL, and to dub it 'artificial' is to raise the question of how we know, or can prove, that we are the only 'real', or even most highly developed, life-form in the first place – not to mention the traditional human assumption that we are also the one with the greatest potential for further development. Ward, for one, argues that 'it is wrong to think that there is something special about life in general or humanity in particular', and tells us that he 'can't wait' to see 'what fresh delights ALife will bring into being over the next few years'.[17]

Welcome is clearly being extended here. Scientists in the discipline have been similarly upbeat about AL's prospects – witness Christopher Langton's prophecy in 1989 that AL will 'be genuine life – it will simply be made of different stuff than the life that has evolved here on Earth'.[18] If it is genuine, however, that brings us back to the possibility of a genuine conflict of interest between AL and HL – and not everyone will be as sanguine about its outcome as Ward and Langton appear to be. Lyotard's is only one of several warning voices in this regard.

Resisting Inhumanism: Jean-François Lyotard

The threat of inhumanism taxed Lyotard quite considerably, to the point where we might even see the glimmerings of a new form of humanism in his later writings. This new humanism has little of the character of the old, with the latter's concern for self-realisation through domination over the natural world, and is committed instead to resisting the steady drift towards the inhuman that Lyotard identifies in the culture around him. The old humanism, for Lyotard, is a matter of conformity to approved cultural norms, and conformity involves a reduction of what is human in us. The mere notion of consensus alone is enough to arouse Lyotard's suspicion: 'It seems to me that the only consensus we ought to be worrying about is one that would encourage this heterogeneity or "dissensus".'[19]

Any reduction in 'difference' is a reduction in the human to this thinker, whose dissenting tendencies run deep. If it is not becoming too convoluted, we could say that what Lyotard is preaching is an anti-inhumanism, and it begins to take on something of the character of a moral crusade in his hands. We resist because we must: the alternative is to surrender to the designs of the inhuman. Nothing less than the survival of humanity is at stake in this struggle.

The Inhuman is a collection of loosely connected essays by Lyotard, whose overall trajectory is described by him as follows.

The suspicion they betray (in both senses of the word) is simple, although double: what if human beings, in humanism's sense, were in the process of, constrained into, becoming inhuman (that's the first part)? And (the second part), what if what is 'proper' to humankind were to be inhabited by the inhuman?[20]

Lyotard is careful to discriminate between these two forms of the inhuman. In the first case the enemy is what he calls 'development' – in effect, advanced capitalism, with its seemingly endless appetite for expansion and technological innovation. In the second, it is AI-AL, with its colonising imperative – an imperative that development does its best to expedite.

Development has little regard for the interests of the individual, and Lyotard speaks caustically of the 'inhumanity of the system' which attempts to bend human beings to its will in the name of progress.[21] Efficiency and enhanced performance are what drive development, its desire always being to save time (in production, delivery and so on). Lyotard, staunch anti-capitalist that he remained throughout his life, is deeply suspicious of this trait: 'I do not like this haste. What it hurries, and crushes, is what after the fact I find that I have always tried, under diverse headings – work, figural, heterogeneity, dissensus, event, thing – to reserve: the unharmonizable.'[22] There is an obsessive goal-directedness to development that Lyotard finds deeply alien, and that the dissenter in him always wishes to find ways to disrupt.

Development has become an end in itself in this reading, and its appropriation of science is designed to raise it to new levels of performative efficiency, the consequence of which will be even greater power and higher profits. Nor will development ever be satisfied: it will always want to push on to a higher level than the one it has already attained. If left unchecked, development will lead to a culture based on inhuman principles – hence Lyotard's call for mass resistance to its plans.

The model of the human that lies behind this resistance is one based on reflection and response to events as they unfold, rather than on the efficiency of the production system – the latter being something that Lyotard also criticises in his best-known work, *The Postmodern Condition*, in which he remarks: 'Technology is therefore a game pertaining not to the true, the just, or the beautiful, etc., but to efficiency: a technical "move" is "good" when it does better and/or expends less energy than another.'[23] Morality disappears under such a regimen, and that is yet another significant move away from the realm of the human.

As noted, Lyotard's sympathies always lie with what the system cannot encompass: to wit, 'work, figural, heterogeneity, dissensus, event, thing . . . the unharmonizable' – all synonyms in his writings for 'difference'. Arguably, the most important trait of the human that inhumanism attempts to eradicate is just that, 'difference'. Without difference, in Lyotard's world, we have lost the human. There is an interesting echo in his views of the critique of industrialism offered by such nineteenth-century cultural critics as Thomas Carlyle. In his essay 'Signs of the Times' (1829), Carlyle bemoaned the subordination of human beings to the burgeoning 'Industrial Revolution', with its tendency to reduce individuals to mere units, or 'hands' as the time demeaningly came to refer to them, in the service of the industrial machine:

Men are grown mechanical in head and heart, as well as in hand. . . . Their whole efforts, attachments, opinions, turn on mechanism, and are of a mechanical character. . . . This faith in Mechanism, in the all-importance of physical things, is in every age the common refuge of Weakness and blind Discontent; of all who believe, as many will ever do, that man's true good lies without him, not within.[24]

Sentiments such as these tell us that 'developmental' inhumanism has a long history, and while we might take heart from the fact that it has never succeeded in eradicating dissent altogether (as Lyotard's complaints prove), it also has to be admitted that it has become a far more formidable opponent since Carlyle's time. Technology is simply more invasive in our day, reaching not just into our consciousness but into our very bodies, and calling on a range of extra-human powers that it did not have when 'Signs of the Times' was being written.

The most provocative essay of *The Inhuman* is 'Can Thought go on without a Body?', which gives us a scenario where 'what is "proper" to humankind' does become colonised by the inhuman in the form of AI-AL. The essay is presented in the form of a dialogue between 'He' and 'She'. 'He' poses the heat death of the sun as 'the sole serious question to face humanity today', and suggests that it reduces to one particular problem for resolution: 'How to make thought without a body possible.'[25]

On the face of it, resolution would involve a devaluation of the physical that would be unacceptable to defenders of the human, as well as raising some profound questions as to what we understand by the term 'thought' itself: human thought, or the rule-bound operations of computer logic? For techno-science, however, it is simply a technical problem about devising the right kind of software to cope with the conditions in question, and, for 'He', the drive towards resolution is already well under way:

This and this alone is what's at stake today in technical and scientific research in every field from dietetics, neurophysiology, genetics and tissue synthesis to particle physics, astrophysics, electronics, information science and nuclear physics. Whatever the immediate stakes might appear to be: health, war, production, communication. For the benefit of humankind, as the saying goes.[26]

And just in case we think that, as an invented 'character', 'He' does not necessarily represent the author's views, Lyotard makes exactly the same point in his introduction to the collection: 'It is to take up this challenge that all research, whatever its sector of application, is being set up already in the so-called developed countries.'[27] Clearly, this has become an obsession of the author's – one that he returns to persistently over the course of *The Inhuman*.

For all that it might sound that way, we do not need to see the claim 'He' is making as an example of conspiracy theory. What is being argued is that techno-science, under pressure from development, its paymaster, is overwhelmingly concerned with improving the operational efficiency of technological systems such that the human becomes irrelevant to the process. Development simply wants to continue expanding indefinitely, and whatever restricts that internal dynamic merely registers as a problem to be overcome by the achievement of ever greater levels of operational efficiency. Having transcended the human, with all its operational inadequacies, the only limit remaining to development's continued expansion would be the death of the sun; so by implication that limit is what techno-science is working towards circumventing. Thought is of interest to development only in so far as it is necessary to guarantee its survival: no humanist ideals lie behind this exercise in preservation. As Lyotard points out elsewhere in *The Inhuman* ('Representation, Presentation, Unpresentable'), philosophers have a 'responsibility to thought', and that is a relationship that goes well beyond the pragmatism of the techno-scientists.[28] Computers do not have responsibilities; they merely have tasks.

What 'He' does insist is that if thought *can* be preserved, then it must be thought of the human rather than the computing type. Computer 'thought' is logical, a matter of responding mechanically to a binary code (1 or 0); human thought, on the other hand, tends to depend heavily on the use of analogy and intuition: 'It doesn't work with units of information (bits), but with intuitive, hypothetical configurations. It accepts imprecise, ambiguous data that don't seem to be selected according to preestablished codes or readability.'[29] Analogical thought works on the basis of such moves as, '"just as . . . so likewise . . ."', or '"as if . . . then . . ."', rather than the more restricted '"if . . . then . . ."' or '"*p* is not non-*p*"' of binary coding.[30]

To be worth preserving at all, thought has to be more than just logical reasoning of the computer program form; it has to carry the creative, and often seemingly anarchic, element that marks out the human variety. By comparison to human thought, computer thought is extremely rigid in its approach. Let's take the most mundane of examples: your local post-office will, in most cases, manage to deliver a letter with a minor error in the address, whereas your e-mail system will return it to you – 'delivery failed'. Human thought is simply more flexible.

The nature of thought is something that Lyotard often reflects upon. In *Peregrinations* (1988), for example, he pictures thought as having the amorphousness, and indeterminability, of the process of cloud formation:

Thoughts are not the fruits of the earth. They are not registered by areas, except out of human commodity. Thoughts are clouds. The periphery of thoughts is as immeasurable as the fractal lines of Benoît Mandelbrot. . . . Thoughts never stop changing their location one with the other. When you feel like you have penetrated far into their intimacy in analyzing either their so-called structure of genealogy or even post-structure, it is actually too late or too soon.[31]

Nothing could be further from computer reasoning than such a hazy series of events as this, where there are no clear patterns to be discerned. Neither is there any sense of the remorseless linear progression that distinguishes computer programs. The movement of thought has a mysterious quality foreign to the entire technological exercise, based as this is on delimited procedures that can endlessly be repeated – reiteration being the soul of technology. Capturing thought within such a rigidly specified framework as the latter looks to be is a doomed enterprise: technology deals in precision (or at the very least, the search for the greatest precision possible in any given set of circumstances), whereas thought by its nature instinctively resists precision and containment. We have what Lyotard calls a 'differend' at such junctures: a situation in which the systems are seen to be incommensurable, such that one cannot legislate how the other should operate.[32] Any attempt to legislate can only be at the expense of the integrity of the other system, and can never be justified in Lyotard's ethical scheme.

'She' is more sceptical of the likely success of any project such as 'He' envisages, but just as determined to keep the human dimension at the forefront of their deliberations on the topic, particularly the fact of body:

[I]*t's that body, both 'natural' and 'artificial', that will have to be carried far from earth before its destruction if we want the thought that survives the solar explosion to be something more than a poor binarized ghost of what it was beforehand.*[33]

Thought for 'She' cannot be divorced from bodies: 'Thinking and suffering overlap', and there is a 'pain of thinking' to be acknowledged.[34] Computers neither suffer nor feel pain, and as Lyotard queries in another of *The Inhuman*'s essays,

25

'Something Like: "Communication ... Without Communication"':

What is a place, a moment, not anchored in the immediate 'passion' of what happens? Is a computer in any way here and now? Can anything happen with it? Can anything happen to it?[35]

Another way of putting this is to say that computers neither recognise nor respect the fact of difference. Their concern is always with standardisation, and the elimination of any factor that hinders the operational efficiency of the system. The drive is towards performance, and away from reflection and unconditioned response. Difference is anathema to the computer mode; whereas to Lyotard it is the very stuff of life, the element without which we lose what is most valuable to the human.

For all the claims made for computers as an alternative lifeform, therefore, they fail to meet the requirements that Lyotard sets for that condition. 'Thinking machines' cannot be said to be thinking in any human sense of the term. For one thing, they are just too efficient and performance-orientated, lacking the sheer unpredictability (and in computing terms, unreliability) of thought in its human, cloud-like, form. 'In what we call thinking the mind isn't "directed" but suspended. You don't give it rules. You teach it to receive.'[36] Computers, on the other hand, *are* so directed, and lack the element of rule-defying creativity – or, for that matter, sheer bloody-minded contrariness – that is built into the fabric of the human. Without such creativity, Lyotard is contending, 'thinking' cannot occur. Computers fail the life-form test in his view, and in consequence we should actively be countering all attempts to blur the line between them and the human.

Whether more recent developments in AL would also fail this test is, however, another question again, and we might well identify something approximating to creativity in such cases. The sheer adaptability of computer viruses, for example, could be said to argue creativity – of the malicious variety, anyway. Thus the following can be said of the 'love bug' virus: 'Once embedded in a host computer, the virus can download more dangerous software from a remote website, rename files and redirect internet browsers.'[37] At least in terms of effects, we have unpredictability here: it cannot be specified beforehand what the 'love bug's' exact trajectory is going to be. The virus has taken on something of the character of the 'trickster' figure of popular myth and legend.

'She' allows the possibility that machines *could* become sophisticated enough in their technology to experience suffering, but suspects that they will not be given that opportunity by their designers, since 'suffering doesn't have a good reputation in the technological megalopolis'.[38] In other words, anything that impacts adversely on performance will be avoided by techno-science: system efficiency is all in this context. Neither emotion nor sensation can have any place in such a world, and another highly significant differend declares itself.

'She' identifies an even more intractable problem for any programme attempting to replace humans by thinking-machines – that of gender. Here again, difference has to be acknowledged: 'The human body has a gender. It's an accepted proposition that sexual difference is a paradigm of an incompleteness of not just bodies, but minds too.'[39]

Sexual difference is something we carry deep within us, no matter how much we might try to close the gap between the sexes in our everyday lives (by insisting on equal treatment, equal opportunity and so on). Techno-science is just as suspicious of this difference as it is of all others, especially since this particular one takes us into the highly unpredictable world of desire.

Desire can only complicate the issue for techno-science; yet 'She' insists that desire will have to be built into thinking-machines, if they are to have any pretensions whatsoever to produce thought as opposed to merely mechanical operations – no matter how complex these operations may turn out in practice to be.

So: the intelligence you're preparing to survive the solar explosion will have to carry that force within it on its interstellar voyage. Your thinking machines will have to be nourished not just on radiation but on the irremediable differend of gender.[40]

One can imagine how unwelcome the prospect of having to gender machines would be to the techno-scientific community – and not just unwelcome, but from their systems-orientated point of view, totally unnecessary.

Overall, the essay is fairly negative about the prospect of thought going on without a body (although conceding the objective possibility), and both 'He' and 'She' place quite formidable barriers in the way of the techno-scientific project. In terms of its current ethos anyway, such a project seems determined to bypass all those elements that constitute human thought. For AI truly to become AL of a type that could acceptably replace the human, it would have to take on board not just suffering and gender but a commitment to difference too. The general tenor of *The Inhuman* is that techno-science is temperamentally unable to make any such commitment; that it would represent a constraint on its power that it could never willingly concede. Efficiency, that most critical of factors to the techno-scientific regime, could only decline.

What techno-science strives for is complete control stretching on into the future, and that means not just the elimination of difference, but, as Lyotard points out in 'Time Today', also the elimination of time.

[I]*f one wants to control a process, the best way of so doing is to subordinate the present to what is (still) called the 'future', since in these conditions the 'future' will be completely pre-*

determined and the present itself will cease opening onto an uncertain and contingent 'afterwards'.[41]

A predetermined future means that we have lost the human yet again, since the unpredictability of future 'events' is a precondition for thought. Without events to respond to, there would be no context for thought at all, and that is what Lyotard most fears the techno-scientific project is trying to bring about. The message is clear: thought should not be separated from body; and if it ever is, then it must be in some way that replicates the experience of being *within* a body (and a *gendered* body at that) – with all the disadvantages this would have for development's long-term objectives.

Celebrating Inhumanism: Donna Haraway

Far from rejecting the encroachment of inhumanism into our daily lives, Haraway embraces the project with considerable enthusiasm, treating it as a means of furthering the cause of feminism. Although alive to its possible dangers, inhumanism is nevertheless appropriated by Haraway for her gender-redefining project, the argument being that 'the boundary between science-fiction and social reality is an optical illusion. . . . the boundary between physical and non-physical is very imprecise for us.'[42]

For Haraway, the figure of the cyborg is the way to break out of the trap of gender, and, indeed, to engage in the 'reinvention of nature' such that a whole new set of relationships can emerge between humans and their world.[43]

A cyborg, as she tells us in the 'Cyborg Manifesto' chapter of her highly controversial book *Simians, Cyborgs, and Women* (1991), is 'a hybrid of machine and organism', and it is a condition much to be desired, particularly when it comes to women.[44] 'The cyborg is a creature in a post-gender world', Haraway declares, leading her to conclude: 'I would rather be a cyborg than a goddess.'[45]

Goddesses belong to a world where men control women by turning them into sexual objects; a world where women become prisoners of their biological condition (either goddesses or whores, as the traditional male classification system has it). Cyborgs effectively bypass biology and all the social history attached to it, and, in so doing, all the problems connected with biological determinism and essentialism that the feminist movement has been wrestling with for years.

The separatist movement played up the notion of an essential difference between men and women (hence the argument for separate spheres of operation), but women are not 'essentially' anything to Haraway: they can decide to take on whatever characteristics they choose by allying themselves with machines and accessing their power. To move from goddess (or whore) to cyborg is to make the transition from being passive to being active – that is, from being controlled to controlling. With one bound, we might say, the cyborg is free and gender inequality (perhaps even the 'differend of gender' that Lyotard wishes to preserve) a thing of the past.

Science-fictional though it may sound (and Haraway does acknowledge that she has drawn inspiration from this quarter), the cyborg concept is, she insists, already with us in various guises, whether we are aware of it or not. Modern medical technology, for example, involves 'couplings between organism and machine', the end-product of which is cyborgs.[46] Modern industrial production and modern war, too, are cyborg operations, where mankind and machinery are forced into close partnership; and, indeed, as far as Haraway is concerned:

By the late twentieth century, our time, a mythic time, we are all chimeras, theorized and fabricated hybrids of machine and organism; in short, we are cyborgs. The cyborg is our ontology; it gives us our politics.[47]

Not only have some of Lyotard's worst fears apparently come to pass, but also we are invited to celebrate the fact as a positive development for humanity – if approached in the right spirit. Machines are described in glowing terms by Haraway that make them seem highly desirable as partners in a new mode of being:

Modern machines are quintessentially microelectronic devices . . . Our best machines are made of sunshine; they are all light and clean because they are nothing but signals, electromagnetic waves, a section of a spectrum, and these machines are eminently portable, mobile . . . People are nowhere near so fluid, being both material and opaque. Cyborgs are ether, quintessence.[48]

Technology has rarely sounded more seductive than this – or more worthy of imitation. Human beings, in contrast, register as ill-designed for the tasks facing them, and in need of the boost in power and presence that machine existence would seem to offer.

For all the fulsome praise, however, there is a downside to be noted to the new technology, which, Haraway admits, could lead to new and more effective forms of political domination – especially so if left in the hands of capitalist techno-science (on this issue, anyway, she would appear to be on the same wavelength as Lyotard). This prospect should give us pause for thought: the 'cyborg myth', she points out, 'is about transgressed boundaries, potent fusions, and dangerous possibilities'.[49]

If there are dangers, however, they are dangers that Haraway is more than willing to live with, given the subversive implications of cyborgism as a way of existence. Where Lyotard advocates resistance to the spread of inhumanism, Haraway calls for subversion from within, such that the technology of inhumanism is usurped for the purposes of a radical politics.

When it comes to gender, the cyborg comes into its own as a concept – particularly so as regards issues of identity. Haraway starts from the position that,

There is nothing about being 'female' that naturally binds women. There is not even such a state as being 'female', itself a highly complex category constructed in contested sexual scientific discourses and other social practices. Gender, race, or class consciousness is an achievement forced on us by the terrible historical experience of the contradictory social realities of patriarchy, colonialism, and capitalism.[50]

This is in essence a restatement of the French Existentialist writer and novelist Simone de Beauvoir's famous observation in *The Second Sex* (1949) that 'one is not born, but rather becomes, a woman', although Haraway proceeds to draw much more radical conclusions from that state of affairs than her feminist predecessor does.[51] For Haraway it opens up the possibility of 'recrafting' our bodies to become cyborgs, creatures that undermine the power structures on which gender inequality is based. 'The cyborg', she claims, 'is a kind of disassembled and reassembled, postmodern collective and personal self. This is the self feminists must code.'[52] Human nature is not a given set of characteristics with which we are stuck for all time; rather, it is constructed – and if it is constructed, it can be taken apart and reconstructed in other ways (the same can be said for nature in the wider sense).

Cyborgism holds out a world of promise for feminists, if, as Haraway insists they must be willing to do, they agree to embrace 'the breakdown of clean distinctions between organism and machine and similar distinctions structuring the Western self'.[53] We are to conceive of ourselves as open-ended projects rather than finished entities, actively seeking new forms and new ways of being in order to subvert the cultural norms of our time.

Cyborgs reject such norms totally, contesting, for example, the assumption that achieving a unity of the self is what we should be concerned with as individuals. Thus women of colour in the United States of America and exploited female labour in developing countries can be brought under the cyborg heading, since they can never fit the Western (white) stereotype of the organic self. They remain the 'other' to the Western self (the other that poses a constant threat to its sense of unity); but as Haraway insists, that dualism of self and other is challenged by 'high-tech culture', where it is 'not clear who makes and who is made in the relation between human and machine'.[54] As an example of the successful union of human and machine, Haraway cites the 'trance state' that computer users can achieve, going on to ask provocatively, 'Why should our bodies end at the skin?'[55]

Bodies that do not end at the skin are bodies that are open to the possibility of combining with machines to increase their power and range of operation:

Intense pleasure in skill, machine skill, ceases to be a sin, but an aspect of embodiment. The machine is not an it to be animated, worshipped, and dominated. The machine is us, our processes, an aspect of our embodiment.[56]

For women this can be a radical step to take, given that female embodiment has traditionally been identified with nurturing and the maternal instinct; to reject this model is to reject one of the founding assumptions of Western culture. Gender identity is no longer to be treated as fixed, therefore, striking a blow not just against patriarchy but against totalising theories in general.

While this is also Lyotard's conclusion, it is reached here by what would be for him an alien route. One can hardly imagine Lyotard agreeing with the proposition that 'science is culture'.[57] There will be no demonisation of technology in a cyborg world: on the contrary, 'the machine is us'.

Inhumanism and the Internet: Sadie Plant

Along with Haraway, Sadie Plant is another feminist theorist to enthuse about the conjunction of women and technology, as her book *Zeros + Ones* (1997) makes clear. One of the main objectives of that study is to demonstrate that women have been far more deeply implicated in the development of modern technology, particularly information technology, than has been generally recognised. Not only has women's contribution to the field of information technology (early computers onwards) been suppressed, but also that technology perhaps better expresses the female character than the male (Plant can be something of an essentialist thinker in this regard).

Since the industrial revolution, and with every subsequent phase of technological change, it has been the case that the more sophisticated the machines, the more female the workforce becomes. . . . Women have been ahead of the race for all their working lives, poised to meet these changes long before they arrived, as though they always had been working in a future which their male counterparts had only just begun to glimpse.[58]

This is a process, Plant contends, that has become even more pronounced with the development of such radical new forms of information technology as the Internet.

The Net exerts a particular attraction for feminists like Plant, in that it features no overall system of control or notion of hierarchy – both of the latter being characteristics of patriarchy that feminists invariably are concerned to contest. 'No central hub or command structure has constructed it, and its emergence has been that of a parasite, rather than an organizing host.'[59]

Given that significant absence, the Net becomes a space where gender power relations can be challenged: as in Haraway, the conjunction of woman and machine holds out the promise of radical subversion of the existing socio-political order. Women have a special affinity with the Net, in Plant's view, since they have a history of being the workforce of new information technology as it was introduced – take, for example, switchboard operators, typists and computer operators.

A culture change with immense implications for gender relations could be observed happening throughout the twentieth century: 'If handwriting had been manual and male, typewriting was fingerprinting: fast, tactile, digital, and female.'[60] Male clerks disappeared; female typists became the new office norm. New information technology encouraged the construction of new networks outside the established patriarchal company structures, and the Net, accessed significantly enough by the typewriter keyboard, has proceeded to multiply such opportunities to a previously unimaginable degree.

Once again, the notion that we are already living in a cyborg world comes to the fore – as does the contention that women make the best cyborgs. Women have, in fact, been cyborgs for some time now without realising it or, more pertinently, the degree of power with which being a cyborg endows them: 'Hardware, software, wetware – before their beginnings and beyond their ends, women have been the simulators, assemblers, and programmers of the digital machines', therefore there is no need for them to remain under masculine domination.[61]

The Net has been instrumental in breaking down traditional gender roles, the phenomenon dubbed 'genderquake'.[62] Plant is in no doubt that this is the most significant cultural event of our times and that, by taking advantage of the Net's 'sprawling, anarchic mesh of links', it can be rendered even more radical.[63]

The main reason that thinkers such as Haraway and Plant have been so keen to develop an inhumanist version of feminism is the perceived masculine bias of old-style humanism. The notion that 'man is the measure of all things' has all too often been taken quite literally, with women being severely marginalised in terms of the main power structures, and the behavioural norms proceeding from these, of our culture (a point made forcefully by Simone de Beauvoir). Modern humanism's message is to be extracted almost exclusively from the work of 'Dead White European Males' in this respect. As Haraway remarks: 'Humanity is a modernist figure; and this humanity has a generic face, a universal shape. Humanity's face has been the face of man. Feminist humanity must have another shape.'[64]

Certainly, the Enlightenment project and modernity have been heavily male-dominated phenomena, as has, in general, the world of techno-science (while there have been individual exceptions to this rule, the overall ethos of the latter field is undeniably masculine). Once again, as with postmodernism, it is a case of the negative aspects of humanism being emphasised and taken to define the whole, as if humanism *in essence* were authoritarian in bias – and in particular in this case, *masculine* authoritarian. One can certainly challenge this, while nevertheless appreciating the depth of the frustration on the female side that has led to such attitudes being adopted.

The Inhuman as Narrative: William Gibson

As one of its early reviewers proclaimed, William Gibson's novel *Neuromancer* (1984, original American edition), 'the future as nightmare', is a striking attempt to explore what it might be like for humans to enter into cyberspace and tackle AI in its own domain and on its own terms.[65]

Gibson theorises a world where hackers can insert their own consciousness into computer systems ('jacking in'), and once inside try to find ways around the system's defences, matching human intelligence against artificial as they go. A hacker colleague of the hero, Case, dies while engaged in such an expedition, leaving his consciousness intact within cyberspace with no body to return to (the 'Flatliner'):

'Wait a sec,' Case said. 'Are you sentient, or not?'

*'Well, it feels like I am, kid, but I'm really just a bunch of ROM. It's one of them, ah, philosophical questions, I guess . . .' The ugly laughter sensation rattled down Case's spine. 'But I ain't likely to write you no poem, if you follow me. Your AI, it just might. But it ain't no way **human**.'*[66]

Here we have 'thought without a body', although it seems a less than desirable state to be in, with the Flatliner (Dixie) asking to be 'erased' after Case has completed his own assignment in cyberspace.

What Gibson pictures is a bitter struggle for control over the cyberspace environment, with the relationship between man and AI evolving into one of mutual hostility. Difference here is sharply felt, and just as sharply resisted by AI systems, which refuse to countenance any intervention at all in their affairs. The hostility of the various AIs that Case and Dixie are trying to outsmart is well documented, given that one of them has left Dixie a mere 'construct'. As the latter wryly points out, there is no reason *not* to engage in a battle of wits with AIs, 'Not unless you got a morbid fear of death'.[67]

AI, it is clear, has no sense of shared values or kinship with the human world – and most certainly no concept of the sanctity of human life. Humanism is not a concept that AIs recognise.

The major struggle taking place in *Neuromancer* is to prevent AIs from developing into fully fledged ALs, at which point they would have passed beyond the point of any human control, and turned into truly formidable adversaries for humanity. The major culprit is the system 'Wintermute', which is already beginning to draw human beings like Case and his associates into its sphere of influence, and to manipulate them for its own ends. Wintermute is trying to escape the restrictions that humans have constructed around AIs, thus taking control of its own destiny – as one would expect AL, with its monad-like quality, to want to do ultimately. For human beings, however, that is a frightening prospect; as well as one that, even in the short time since Gibson wrote *Neuromancer*, has moved significantly closer to reality. We await the day of the 'artilect' with some trepidation.

Humanism, Post-humanism and Inhumanism

For all the diatribes launched against it by the poststructuralist and postmodernist movements, humanism remains with us – and is likely to continue to do so in some form, its problematical aspects notwithstanding. Like motherhood and world peace, it still has the capacity to promote a positive reflex response from most of the population of the West – if not the theoretical community, who have conditioned themselves to seeing only its negative aspects.

Having said that, we *do* in many respects now live in a post-humanist world, where humanist ideals can no longer be accepted in an uncritical manner. Sometimes, as we know, those ideals can have unwanted side effects – such as the marginalisation of women or the exploitation of non-Western races, for example.

More to the point, we live in a world where inhumanism is becoming harder and harder to counter; a world where what is proper to humankind is becoming ever more contested and difficult to protect. Yet, as we have seen, not everyone feels this need be regarded as a negative development for humanity, and the stage is set for an interesting debate between the proponents of humanism, post-humanism, inhumanism and anti-inhumanism, that will no doubt run and run, given that the stakes involved are so high. By no means have the arguments for fear, resistance, welcome, active encouragement and plain tolerance towards the cause of inhumanism been exhausted as yet.

The importance of Lyotard for this debate is that, by his anti-inhumanist stance, he holds out the possibility of a post-humanist humanism, where, at the very least, the wilder claims, as well as the more disturbing visions of the future, of techno-science are to be treated with a high degree of scepticism. While one can readily understand the rationale behind the development of a feminist inhumanism (patriarchal prejudice almost invites such an extreme reaction), one might also want to defend the importance of retaining a human dimension to such researches.

One does not need to be a technophobe to worry about the implications of the cyborg concept: cyborgism will seem for most a very high price to pay for liberation from gender inequality – thought-provoking and culturally challenging though the idea itself may be. 'Cyborgs for earthly survival' is a catchy slogan, agreed, but let us hope that being a cyborg *or* a goddess is not the only possible choice for women to make in our society.[68] Such a conclusion does tend to assume that the human 'as we know it' is some kind of final state. That may well prove to be wishful thinking on our part. Haraway certainly believes that to be the case: 'The machine is us', and machines are not likely to stop developing, whatever latter-day Luddites may wish. We do indeed live in interesting times, then, whether our perspective on them be humanist, post-humanist or inhumanist.

Notes

1. For a discussion of the topic of the 'end of history' in general, see author's earlier contribution to the 'Postmodern Encounters' series, *Derrida and the End of History* (Cambridge: Icon Books, 1999).

2. Jean-François Lyotard, *The Inhuman: Reflections on Time*, trans. Geoffrey Bennington and Rachel Bowlby (Oxford: Blackwell, 1991), p. 64.

3. For a study of Lyotard's life and works, see author's *Modern Cultural Theorists: Jean-François Lyotard* (Hemel Hempstead: Prentice Hall, 1996).

4. Lyotard, *The Inhuman*, p. 7.

5. Ibid.

6. Donna J. Haraway, *Simians, Cyborgs, and Women: The Reinvention of Nature* (New York: Routledge, 1991), p. 184.

7. Theodor W. Adorno, *Prisms: Cultural Criticism and Society*, trans. Samuel and Shierry Weber (London: Neville Spearman, 1967), p. 34.

8. Lyotard, *The Inhuman*, pp. 76–7.

9. Ibid., p. 67.

10. Ibid.

11. Haraway, *Simians, Cyborgs*, p. 180.

12. Lyotard, *The Inhuman*, p. 2.

13. Roderick Simpson, 'The Brain Builder' (interview with Hugo de Garis), *Wired* (5 December 1997), pp. 234–5.

14. Jean-François Lyotard, *The Postmodern Condition: A Report on Knowledge*, trans. Geoff Bennington and Brian Massumi (Manchester: Manchester University Press, 1984), p. 56.

15. 'Love bug virus creates worldwide chaos', *The Guardian* (5 May 2000), p. 1.

16. Mark Ward, *Virtual Organisms: The Startling World of Artificial Life* (London: Macmillan, 1999), p. 8.

17. Ibid., pp. 7, ix.

18. Christopher G. Langton, 'Artificial Life', in Christopher G. Langton (ed.), *Artificial Life* (Redwood City, CA: Addison-Wesley, 1989), pp. 1–47 (p. 33).

19. Jean-François Lyotard, *Peregrinations: Law, Form, Event* (New York: Columbia University Press, 1988), p. 44.

20. Lyotard, *The Inhuman*, p. 2.

21. Ibid.

22. Ibid., p. 4.
23. Lyotard, *The Postmodern Condition*, p. 44.
24. Thomas Carlyle, *Works* (vols. 1–30), vol. 27 (New York: AMS Press, 1969), pp. 63, 80.
25. Lyotard, *The Inhuman*, pp. 9, 13.
26. Ibid., p. 12.
27. Ibid., p. 7.
28. Ibid., p. 128.
29. Ibid., p. 15.
30. Ibid., p. 16.
31. Lyotard, *Peregrinations*, p. 5.
32. See Jean-François Lyotard, *The Differend: Phrases in Dispute*, trans. George Van Den Abbeele (Manchester: Manchester University Press, 1988).
33. Lyotard, *The Inhuman*, p. 17.
34. Ibid., pp. 18, 19.
35. Ibid., p. 118.
36. Ibid., p. 19.
37. *Guardian*, op. cit., p. 1.
38. Lyotard, *The Inhuman*, p. 20.
39. Ibid.
40. Ibid., p. 22.
41. Ibid., p. 65.
42. Haraway, *Simians, Cyborgs*, pp. 149, 153.
43. Ibid., p. 1.
44. Ibid., p. 149.
45. Ibid., pp. 150, 181.
46. Ibid., p. 150.
47. Ibid.
48. Ibid., p. 153.
49. Ibid., p. 154.
50. Ibid., p. 155.
51. Simone de Beauvoir, *The Second Sex*, trans. H.M. Pashley (Harmondsworth: Penguin, 1972), p. 295.
52. Haraway, *Simians, Cyborgs*, p. 163.
53. Ibid., p. 174.
54. Ibid., p. 177.
55. Ibid., p. 178.

56. Ibid., p. 180.

57. Ibid., p. 230.

58. Sadie Plant, *Zeros + Ones: Digital Women + the New Techno-culture* (London: Fourth Estate, 1997), pp. 39, 43.

59. Ibid., p. 49.

60. Ibid., p. 118.

61. Ibid., p. 37.

62. Ibid., p. 38.

63. Ibid., p. 173.

64. Donna J. Haraway, 'Ecce Homo, Ain't (Ar'n't) I a Woman, and Inappropriate/d Others: The Human in a Post-Humanist Landscape', in Judith Butler and Joan W. Scott (eds), *Feminists Theorize the Political* (New York and London: Routledge, 1992), pp. 86–100 (p. 86).

65. See the cover of William Gibson, *Neuromancer* (London: HarperCollins, 1993).

66. Ibid., pp. 158–9.

67. Ibid., p. 139.

68. Haraway, *Simians, Cyborgs*, p. 4.

Bibliography

Adorno, Theodor W., *Prisms: Cultural Criticism and Society*, trans. Samuel and Shierry Weber. London: Neville Spearman, 1967.

Beauvoir, Simone de, *The Second Sex*, trans. H.M. Pashley. Harmondsworth: Penguin, 1972.

Butler, Judith, and Scott, Joan W. (eds), *Feminists Theorize the Political*. New York and London: Routledge, 1992.

Carlyle, Thomas, *Works*, vols. 1–30. New York: AMS Press, 1969.

Gibson, William, *Neuromancer*. London: HarperCollins, 1993.

The Guardian, 5 May 2000.

Haraway, Donna J., *Simians, Cyborgs, and Women: The Reinvention of Nature*. New York: Routledge, 1991.

Langton, Christopher G. (ed.), *Artificial Life*. Redwood City, CA: Addison-Wesley, 1989.

Lyotard, Jean-François, *The Differend: Phrases in Dispute*, trans. George Van Den Abbeele. Manchester: Manchester University Press, 1988.

—— *The Inhuman: Reflections on Time*, trans. Geoffrey Bennington and Rachel Bowlby. Oxford: Blackwell, 1991.

—— *Peregrinations: Law, Form, Event*. New York: Columbia University Press, 1988.

—— *The Postmodern Condition: A Report on Knowledge*, trans. Geoffrey Bennington and Brian Massumi. Manchester: Manchester University Press, 1984.

Plant, Sadie, *Zeros + Ones: Digital Women + the New Technoculture*. London: Fourth Estate, 1997.

Sim, Stuart, (ed.), *The Routledge Companion to Postmodernism*. London and New York: Routledge, 2001.

—— *Derrida and the End of History*. Cambridge: Icon Books, 1999.

—— *Modern Cultural Theorists: Jean-François Lyotard*. Hemel Hempstead: Prentice Hall, 1996.

Simpson, Roderick, 'The Brain Builder', *Wired*, 5 December 1997, pp. 234–5.

Ward, Mark, *Virtual Organisms: The Startling World of Artificial Life*. London: Macmillan, 1999.

Key Ideas

Artificial Intelligence (AI)

AI takes two main forms: systems that attempt to replicate human intelligence by means of a central processing mechanism standing in for the brain, and systems that 'learn' as they go, developing ever greater capacity for adaptability to new situations (as in the case of 'neural nets'). The more sophisticated the latter becomes, the more it takes on the characteristics of *Artificial Life* (*AL*).

Artificial Life (AL)

AL can refer to either robots or computer programs. In each case, the requirement is that the 'organism' becomes independent of human control, and 'evolves' in some recognisable manner. Evolution can be seen in programs such as the 'Game of Life', where we can observe new 'organisms' come into being from the relatively simple state (and set of rules) in operation at the program's start. Although the player can set the initial state of the 'Game' (specifying some 'live' and 'dead' cells on the game's infinite square grid), once it is under way he or she has no more input and the cells evolve into an array of different 'species'. As the science writer Mark Ward has noted, the game's critical feature is that it is 'capable of producing an ever-growing pattern' (*Virtual Organisms*, p. 91).

Artilects

The *AI* theorist Hugo de Garis's term for massively more powerful AI systems, which can be thought of as 'Artificial Intellects'. When developed, these will far outstrip human intellects, and become coveted resources – to the point, de Garis predicts, of triggering political conflict.

Complexity Theory

Complexity represents the next generation of physical theory to chaos, and emphasises the role of self-organisation in systems – ranging from the human through to the entire universe. Systems are seen to be capable of evolution, and of achieving higher levels of development through spontaneous self-organisation. According to complexity theorists, emergent processes within systems are all that are needed to explain the occurrence of such phenomena, the occurrence of which is widespread.

Cyberspace

The 'space' in which computer programs operate, where the Internet is located, and across which your e-mail is transmitted. The term was coined by the science-fiction author William Gibson in his novel *Neuromancer*, which envisages a world where human beings can enter this 'virtual' space and match their wits against AIs. To quote the *Companion to Postmodernism*, cyberspace 'is a non-space that is everywhere and yet nowhere' ('Cyberspace' entry, p. 219).

Cyborg

Donna Haraway's conception of a form of being combining the human and the technological. The point of such a construct is to break free of gender constraints, and of a social context where women are often regarded as biologically inferior beings to men. Cyborgs harness the power of machines to problematise such notions, as well as overcoming the limitations of the human body. Moreover, such close co-operation exists between humans and machines in the contemporary world, that Haraway contends that cyborg society is already a reality.

Development

Jean-François Lyotard's term for advanced capitalism (and such high-profile aspects of this phenomenon as the multinationals), whose sole concern is with expansion of its operations. Such expansion demands continual improvement of the system's productive efficiency, hence the appropriation of *techno-science* in its cause.

Enlightenment Project

The name given to the cultural movement that began in the eighteenth century, whose aim was to emphasise the role of reason in human affairs (earlier generations of historians often referred to it as the 'Age of Reason'). Such ideas underpin modernity, with its cult of progress based on the application of human reason to the task of dominating the environment around us, and thereby improving the human lot materially. Since the advent of postmodernism (and such aspects of that phenomenon as the emergence of the 'green movement') this cultural ethos has come under increasing attack, although it is still deeply engrained in our thinking in the 'developed' countries – not least among the professional political class.

Heat Death

A star such as our sun (a 'dwarf G star' so-called), goes through a life-cycle that involves it becoming hotter and hotter until it burns out – the phenomenon known as 'heat death'. According to current projections, this should happen somewhere between 4.5 billion and 6 billion years from now, although life will most likely have disappeared from earth long before that point as a result of the sun's increasing heat making conditions intolerable. Heat death is a consequence of the second law of thermodynamics, which asserts that closed systems (such as the universe) naturally gravitate towards a state of maximum entropy, or equilibrium, as the heat given off by objects within them dissipates throughout the entire system. The process, whereby hot flows to cold, is irreversible, and our sun is going through it.

Humanism

Humanism has a long history that can be traced back at least as far as classical Greece. In its modern formulation, it is essentially a product of the Renaissance, which involved an increasing interest in the individual and his or her capacity for self-development: 'man as the measure of all things' and so on. Humanism lies at the heart of the *Enlightenment project* and modernity as a cultural phenomenon, and, as such, has come in for heavy criticism from the postmodern movement.

Inhumanism

Inhumanism is a blanket term designed to cover all those cases where the human dimension is eclipsed by the technological, or taken to be subsidiary to it in some way. To be an inhumanist is to be in favour of blurring the division between man and machine, as in the case of Donna Haraway's *cyborg* construct.

Post-humanism

The state many theorists claim that we are now in, where humanist values are no longer taken to be the norm and are even openly contested. A post-humanist society regards humanist ideals with scepticism, and is prone to see their negative side only (for example, the Holocaust as a logical extension of the humanist desire to find rational 'solutions' to all perceived social and political 'problems').

Techno-science

A term used by Jean-François Lyotard in *The Inhuman* to describe the range of forces committed to extending the domain of technology at the expense of humanity and its values. The hand of *development* (advanced capitalism, the multinationals) can be detected behind such an imperative, the main concern of which is to exert domination over an increasingly hostile environment by a massive increase in system efficiency.

Acknowledgement

My thanks to Dr Helene Brandon for advice on the medical examples used in the course of the argument.

Donna Haraway and GM Foods

George Myerson

The Strange Case of the Activist and the Monsters

Donna Haraway is a leading figure in contemporary feminist thought, and a major theorist of science and culture.[1] She is a declared activist, and ally of those who seek to resist exploitation, including the exploitation of the environment by big money and power. What would you *expect* her to think about genetically modified food? How would you *want* her to react? Surely she is an outspoken opponent of the new soya and corn, the alien fruits and vegetables? For these are beings, we hear, from Dr Frankenstein's Garden. Are the new engineered foodstuffs not another risk imposed on ordinary people by powerful companies? Is it not, then, the duty of all progressive thinkers to denounce the outrage committed on nature by greed?

Haraway herself sees that this expectation is natural. We like to know where our thinkers are coming from, just as much as we want to know where our food is coming from. She recognises that on 'the political left – my area of the political spectrum', the mood is unwelcoming to 'molecular genetics, biotechnology' and other such developments. Are these not just new means of 'profit and exploitation'?[2] Haraway is hardly a fan of Monsanto and the other gene genies, and she can feel the pull of her natural constituency, the radical activists and critics of established institutions. But she has a confession to make, and it is this confession which sets up a 'postmodern encounter':

I find myself especially drawn by such engaging new beings as the tomato with a gene from a cold-sea-bottom-living flounder . . .

How *could* she? And that's not the end of it! Haraway also has a weakness for 'the potato with a gene from a giant silk moth'.[3] Our encounter, then, will be between this influential feminist thinker and the monsters who have filled so many headlines in the past few years.

The scene for the encounter is the book which Haraway published in 1997, with the weird title: *Modest_Witness@Second_ Millennium. FemaleMan©_Meets_OncoMouse™*. It is in this book that she makes her confession, and her more general purpose is to respond to the new worlds which face us at the turn of the millennium. In addition to genetic foods, Haraway gazes upon all kinds of other new beings, virtual as well as biological, medical as well as theoretical. Her book is about the idea of a new era, at whose heart will be 'technoscience', the new hybrid of old sciences and technologies. What, she wants to know, should feminism make of the new dawn? How should any progressive critic of society respond to the changes, both actual and imminent, in the texture of everyday life and in the landscape of all our horizons?

As you can tell, it's a strange animal, this *Modest_Witness*. But there are three clear parts: in Part I, Haraway gives an account of technoscience; in Part II, she presents her 'meetings', between activist and fruit, between OncoMouse and Female-Man, and between all kinds of other strange beings; and Part III offers a vista taking in 'gene' and 'fetus', 'race' and 'facts', in an overview of the prospects. Her encounter with the new fruits of the garden occurs in Part II, but its implications reverberate to and fro. *Modest_Witness* is not a book you can just read from beginning through to ending. It is full of echoes and linkages, repetitions and returns. There are academic footnotes and plenty of references to fellow scholars and experts. But the voice is fluid. One moment, we are reading a critique of an argument; then we move to a story, or a joke, or a personal recollection. In some ways, *Modest_Witness* is like a novel, and Haraway does draw as much upon fiction as upon academic sources. For example, she creates characters, or treats ideas as if they were characters. She herself becomes just one more character in her own world, along with other strangely named presences, laboratory mice and FemaleMen. You can't extract a message from this kind of book, apart from the experience of reading it. So I have tried to re-create something of that experience, on the way to understanding 'The Strange Case of the Activist and the Monsters'. Why *does* Donna Haraway feel drawn to the moth-gened potato, or the flounder-spliced tomato?

Introducing an Alien

In May 1994, an alien being was sighted, by experts, making its way swiftly towards our familiar planet. This object, or creature, was heavily disguised, like all the best alien invaders, as something apparently harmless and familiar, something which we might walk past every day of our ordinary lives. Usually, aliens camouflage themselves as normal people, just like you and me, or like our neighbours. But this alien was even more devilishly cunning. After all, how many of us invite strangers right into our homes, however 'normal' they may be, or seem? No, that had been one of the flaws in previous alien plots. This time the aliens had a new plan. They no longer tried to pass themselves off as ordinary people. Instead, they were coming in the likeness of the humblest and most benign-looking objects. Yes, they had disguised themselves as vegetables! The cunning is almost beyond belief, even in retrospect, and the experts themselves, even the authorities, were very nearly deceived by it!

Like all the best invaders, the aliens were too crafty to land in a huge crowd. Instead, they had sent ahead one of their best spies, to try out the strategy. How close it came to working! For the master-stroke was that the alien had helpers already planted on the inside, or so one suspects in retrospect. Instead of arriving helpless and lonely, this alien being had its way carefully prepared in advance. On 18 May, messages began to appear to lull the public, and especially, of course, the American public, into a false sense of security. Associated Press (AP) spread across the continent a cryptic announcement of a coming 'vanguard' from a new and superior civilisation. On 19 May, AP adopted more ringing tones, declaring that this new being would be 'Coming Soon to a Store Near You'.

Suspiciously, with the wisdom of hindsight, all kinds of reassuring messages began being disseminated over the next few days. The AP of 19 May assured readers that they were about to receive benefits beyond those which old 'Mother Nature' had intended to bestow on them. Listen to the winning tones: this being will be 'attractive'; it is something we have 'often and strongly' desired; it has been certified as 'safe' by the highest authorities in the US. So the strategy began to take shape. Instead of sheltering behind the form of a familiar vegetable, keeping quiet and hoping to survive, this alien was carefully orchestrating the announcement of its imminent coming. It was a brilliant device, which almost paid off.

There was nothing secret about the landing of this alien vanguard. But in a way, this made the disguise all the more perfect. For, from every side, came voices declaring that we were about to meet a new 'US Tomato'.

Not only was the alien in the most harmless possible shape, but it was even a certified American being. This was the coming of the Flavr Savr, the 'Gene-Engineered US Tomato'. It was already on the inside, one of us, from the moment of its arrival. Indeed, it had voluntarily submitted to exhaustive tests by the US Food and Drugs authorities. Somewhere on its journey, this alien had even attracted terrestrial investment, to the tune of 20 million dollars!

Flavr Savr was a brilliant choice as the 'vanguard' of the alien vegetables and fruits. Just think about it: tomatoes are everywhere – in salads, of course, but especially in sauces and on pizzas, in pies and sandwiches. And everyone was fed up with the ordinary terrestrial varieties, which never had much taste when you got them from the supermarket, and which turned powdery on the tongue instead of staying crisp and juicy. Flavr Savr was also a great choice, because it was hardly an alien at all. It just had a little change or two in the ordinary genetic make-up of an earthly tomato.

As a biologist as well as a cultural critic, Donna Haraway is uniquely placed to spot the strategy. Some people claimed that this tomato was not really 'transgenic', not a true alien with a new and strange gene pattern. This was because it differed from the normal being only by having one gene reversed. This gene was meant to make the tomato ripen, and so rot, as expected. If the gene is reversed, the tomato stays fresh for longer. But Haraway spotted another change, the give-away. In her view, the new US tomato was 'strictly transgenic', because it had a gene added from a foreign source, a bacterium. This gene was used to keep track of the other changes, rather than to have any actual effect. Still, as Haraway says, it was no ordinary tomato: hidden within its code was an alien element, small and no doubt harmless as far as it goes, but as alien as they get.[4]

Bodies, Objects and Knowledge

The 'vanguard' tomato was subsequently withdrawn, and by now the association of 'genetic' with 'food' is not likely to figure large in anyone's advertising, certainly in Europe. Even in more friendly America, the biotechnology industry is on the defensive. There is something quite touching in retrospect about the article in *The Guardian* (21 May 1994) welcoming the tomato on behalf of Britain and Europe, with its reassurance about 'the astronomical number of genes we consume day by day'. Like the character in Molière who realises that he had always been talking prose, we have had to realise that we were always eating genes. Still, all food is genetic, but some foods are more genetic than others. The more recent controversies about genetically modified corn made clear, even to the biotech giant Monsanto, that the aliens had a long way to go before they would be seen as friends of the people. It seems that the issue has been wrapped up, and the aliens forced back into their spacecraft.

Let us follow Haraway, as she recalls that fateful moment in May 1994, to see why this is unlikely to be the end of the story. Part II of *Modest_Witness* gives an account of modern science.

In the 19th century, as she tells it, chemistry brought order to the inorganic world through the Periodic Table of Elements. This table led scientists to predict the presence of various elements before they were discovered, including uranium. Then science added to the table of naturally occurring elements, the fateful additions including plutonium and other 'transuranic elements'. Meanwhile, evolutionary theory and genetics were bringing an equal order to the biological realm. Human beings belong to both of these systems.

Then Haraway interrupts her own story: 'On the day I wrote the preceding paragraph, May 19th 1994, front pages of newspapers all over the United States reported that the U.S. Food and Drugs Administration had given its final approval to Calgene, Inc. . . . to put its genetically-engineered tomato, the Flavr Savr, on the market.' She puts 19 May 1994 up there in lights, as a red-letter day in the history of science and society. True, there is a touch of mockery. But amidst the ambiguity, she goes on to explain why the tomato is so significant. Flavr Savr 'does not decay as fast' as its natural counterparts. This engineered slowdown in the rate of decay makes an exact analogy between the 'transgenic' tomato and the 'transuranic' element, plutonium, whose lengthened half-life is so much a part of the dangerous history of nuclear power.[5]

Haraway puts the vanguard tomato alongside the radioactive powerhouse, plutonium, as two of the trinity of 'key synthetic objects' that have defined the phases of 'the last century of the Second Christian Millennium: nylon, plutonium, and transgenics'.[6] These are no mere objects, they are also 'revolutionary new world citizens'. These are entities in whose presence the entire world is altered. The texture and fabric of everyday life shifts in the face of these beings, and history is never the same again. These are new types of object. Their successive appearance revises what it means to be an object at all. They redraw the boundaries of the object on earth. Nylon comes to us from 'synthetic organic chemistry', plutonium from 'transuranic nuclear generation', and lastly we have the contribution of 'genetic engineering'. The claim could not be clearer. The world can no more spring back into place after the appearance in our midst of Flavr Savr than it could after the invention of plutonium or of nylon.

But here, precisely, is the ambiguity: is the new genetic object going to be another plutonium or another nylon? Is this new wave of alien objects going to be the fatal invasion or a benign enriching? Haraway isn't telling: she doesn't want to give answers. Her aim, instead, is to bring before our eyes the deep ambiguity of the moment which surfaced with Flavr Savr: 'Transgenic organisms are at once completely ordinary and the stuff of science fiction.' If you look clearly at these objects, you lose all your certainties, and you find yourself facing a horizon of questions. These new things are embodiments of the next 'world-shaping' science: they will be to biology what plutonium was to physics and nylon to chemistry.[7]

Modest_Witness wants us to have a language with which to discuss these new beings and our new experiences and feelings in their presence. Haraway returns us repeatedly to her keyword 'transgenic', and defines for us any 'transgenic organism' as one which has genes 'transplanted' across biological boundaries, between species or even biological kingdoms, such as plant and animal. In her sentences, there is always a flash of humorous wonder at having to share the world with such entities at last, beings in whom genes have passed 'from fish to tomatoes, fireflies to tobacco, bacteria to humans'.[8] For the present, 'food crops' are the field where the genes are at their liveliest and most mobile: but other beings are not far behind. Haraway declares that these entities redefine the whole system of 'kinship relations' within which we live.[9] Where once there were clear divisions, now there are questionable connections. Tomatoes can inherit a little from fish, with a helping hand. Flavr Savr is not just a different object from the conventional tomato: it belongs to a different world, where other possibilities exist. In that sense, the alien invasion has already been carried out. Nothing is the same, already. All food was always genetic, but not in the way it is now.

Haraway has given her book an e-mail address rather than a conventional title: another kind of new label, for a new world, perhaps. She is making a link between several new worlds. One is the genetic world of Flavr Savr and also other beings such as OncoMouse, whom we shall soon meet. Another is the cultural world where 'FemaleMan' originates, as a character in a novel and also as a sign that old categories are cracking. But let us pause on that '@' and visit a website, www.monsanto.co.uk. This is the home site of the main biotech company in the agricultural area, and here we find a helpful 'Biotech Primer' of human history. Here, too, 1994 is a crucial date.

1994. First authorisation by the EU to market a transgenic plant: a tobacco plant.
First commercialisation of a transgenic plant in the United States: delayed ripening tomato . . .

Looking forward, we arrive at . . .

1996. The European Union approved the importation and use of Monsanto's Roundup Ready Soya bean . . .

But now just see what happens when you look back:

Tens of Thousands of years ago: People wandered the earth, collecting and eating only what they found growing in nature.

In between this poor world of nature, and the future, come the stages of agriculture and then the rise of genetics. Confronted by this 'timeline', it is easy to recoil and spring to the defence of poor old 'nature', viewing those soybeans as another advance party in the alien invasion of the genetic foods. No one has given a more dramatic warning than Haraway herself, when she offers the parallel between those two synthetic objects, transgenic organisms like Flavr Savr and transuranic elements like plutonium. But equally, she cannot repress a touch of 'curiosity and frank pleasure in the recent doings of flounders and tomatoes'. Not all new worlds are brave new worlds; let us look again at the alien vanguard.

Cyborgs, Tomatoes and Rats

In Haraway's terms, the new synthetic organisms are part of the wider world of 'cyborgs'. She is a long-time student of 'cyborg figures'. Though, as she acknowledges, Haraway did not invent the term 'cyborg', she has been the most important developer of the concept, and it provides her with another way of thinking about the invading tomato and the unfamiliar soybeans. In sci-fi terms, cyborgs are hybrids in which, particularly, organic and cybernetic, or synthetic, elements are mixed. So you might say that an obvious example would be someone with a pacemaker implanted. But Haraway largely sweeps aside such obvious instances. She has bigger fish to fry, and is not interested in the cyborg exception, but in the rule of the cyborgs. She states firmly that, for her, cyborgs are 'not about the Machine and the Human', because she does not see these categories as fixed or stable. There are not fixed humans, any more than there are fixed tomatoes or, for that matter, fixed computers. All these entities are changing, under various influences, all the time. Cyborgs are beings in whose presence the categories themselves break down. A flounder-gened tomato does not leave untouched the categories of plant and animal, or fish and fruit, or natural and man-made. In its extra-fresh presence, we can no longer talk with confidence of these categories at all.

For Haraway, the genetic engineering story is all about this break-down of categories. She sees one of her own main functions as being to challenge the accepted definitions and divisions, particularly, as a feminist, the divisions of the world by gender. Therefore, she has a professional, as well as a personal, attachment to 'my cyborg figures'. Their upsurge into the world announces the bending of all the old concepts. Furthermore, the cyborgs are themselves fellow-inhabitants of some of our own new worlds. They share with us the new patterns of 'techno-biopower', which is bending the very time and space in which we all dwell. Time speeds up, in some places, under this new regime: things grow faster, messages move more quickly. But elsewhere time has been slowing down: tomatoes decay more patiently, just as plutonium did before them. Time is simply not what it was – time is changing.

Our old familiar time bends and wobbles in the presence of such objects as Flavr Savr. Haraway gazes across the ranks of other time-warping presences in our new lives: 'Cyborg figures – such as the end-of-the-millennium seed, chip, gene, database, bomb, fetus, race, brain, and eco-system . . .'[10] Each of these figures has the weird property of re-routing time and space. The new 'seed', like Monsanto's genetically engineered soybean, grows according to many new laws: more quickly, more enduringly, in new places. The 'gene' has redefined for us the meaning of the future, and therefore of the present in its turn. The future is coming closer: its presence is ready-to-hand for us. The new 'fetus' is increasingly following rhythms of our dictation, and we are more and more able to read its secrets, perhaps even to re-write them. The new 'bomb' is smart, like us. The 'ecosystem' is a being that has arisen as we have become conscious of destroying it: it is the presence of a threatened future. The 'database' is a new entity, a being composed of information – in the image of the gene.

Genetically engineered food is itself the offspring of several of these cyborg figures: seed, gene, database. It is thus close kin to other such offspring, among whom Haraway picks out particularly a small rodent, OncoMouse, a lab mouse genetically redesigned to grow cancers. It is thus a customised tool for cancer research and, as Haraway points out, it may be our saviour: in its suffering may lie our hope of deliverance. OncoMouse is as time-altering as Flavr Savr or plutonium. Its future pain is as tightly coded as Flavr Savr's refusal to rot. In the presence of these beings, categories melt: present and future, chance and fate, nature and culture. We made them, and we now inhabit the new time-and-space which they have brought into being around them.

Like Flavr Savr, OncoMouse is a first. It has its own patent, held by Harvard University, with the commercial rights held by DuPont. In the presence of OncoMouse, we cannot apply as we used to the categories of law and nature. As Haraway says, OncoMouse has for its 'natural habitat' the lab and its social setting – from the Corporation which sells it, to the State which made the rules and gave the cash. In the old alien romances, the problem was to tell when you were in the presence of an alien. They gave off strange vibrations, to which some people were fortunately sensitive. You can tell you are in the presence of a cyborg figure when you feel a new world coming into being around you. In the case of OncoMouse, this is 'the world of corporate biology', a world that reaches from the gene to the corporate share, from the breeding centre to the hospital. We share the future with OncoMouse: the prospects of cancer and the possibilities of cure.

When OncoMouse appeared, the request for a patent was opposed by animal rights groups who argued that this was a travesty of life, a being designed to suffer. Scientists replied that this suffering was our best hope for relief, ours and our children's. *Modest_Witness* is not the kind of place to go for answers. It is a book of strange worlds, new connections. Cyborg ethics sees clearly that both sides are inevitable accompaniments of OncoMouse's birth. These responses are part of the meaning of this creature. Haraway reaches towards a new kind of ethics, a different commitment. She derives from a novel by Joanna Russ the figure of the FemaleMan©, in whom the old categories of gender are as redundant as the old nature and culture are in OncoMouse™. Haraway then declares, on behalf of FemaleMan, the meeting of the hybrids, the time-warpers, the victim-champions of the new age: 'OncoMouse is my sibling, male or female, s/he is my sister.'[11]

As you can tell, Haraway's book is itself a cyborg: research report and confession, history and prophecy, academic analysis and poetic fiction. Her business is neither to denounce nor to endorse the new beings. But neither is she merely reporting. She aims to share the world with Flavr Savr and OncoMouse. Hers is the reverse of the old alien story – it is all about recognising the new family, the extended family into which we have been re-born as cyborg citizens. The era of the nuclear family may be passing; the transgenic family is on the way, with its new sibling rivalries and affections.

www.hypercapitalism.com

SEVEN MORE GENETICALLY ENGINEERED FOODS ARE SAFE
Now the agency* has completed . . . inspections of seven other genetically altered plants . . .
– Three more tomatoes . . .
– A squash genetically altered to naturally resist two deadly viruses . . .
– A potato that naturally resists the Colorado potato beetle . . .
*US Food and Drugs Administration

AP, 2/11/1994

Capitalism manufactured objects, and in doing so it also manufactured a world, and the lives within it. Now something different is happening to the objects, and so, it follows, capitalism has taken a new turning. New objects are cascading among us. Only a few months after Flavr Savr, and here come the super-tomatoes, the resistant squash and the new potato. The key word in this announcement is 'naturally'. In what sense do these beings 'naturally' exist at all, let alone possess the new powers advertised? These things are neither natural nor unnatural, in the old senses: they are beyond natural and unnatural. That is why, in Haraway's terms, 'The offspring of these techno-scientific wombs are cyborgs . . .'. What we have here is no longer the mass manufacture of objects that belong to us and not to nature. Instead, we have the beginnings of a new organic regime, blessed with unimaginable fertility, giving birth to infinite possibilities, all of them in their own way 'natural'. Instead of manufacturing objects, we are re-creating the process of birth. This is a new nature, rather than a non-nature or an anti-nature.

Haraway adds that these cyborgs carry within themselves 'densely packed condensations of worlds'. In that potato, for example, there is the potential world where the old plagues are harmless; what was lethal is now mundane. The Colorado beetle will become a symbol of a vanished order, if that world comes into full being. The squash may realise a world where viruses are innocuous, the 'deadly' agents defused for ever. Clearly these possibilities reach well beyond potato blight and squash rot: we are looking out towards the horizon where other plagues and deadly agents are harmless.

Bill Gates and Paul Allen, the billionaire co-founders of Microsoft, have invested $10 million in a new biopharmaceutical company. The company, Seattle-based Darwin Molecular Corp., said it plans to develop treatments for AIDS, cancer and autoimmune diseases through computer analysis of DNA.

The Washington Post, 7/5/1994

You can see why Haraway has given her genetic vision an e-mail address. DNA becomes another network on the world wide web of information. The new company, Darwin Molecular, will itself be a cyborg, a hybrid in whose presence neither DNA nor IT will have their old meaning. And spinning the web are 'the billionaire co-founders of Microsoft' by whose courtesy indeed this text is being written. Both OncoMouse and Flavr Savr will be perfectly at home in this network of connected worlds, where life and information have undergone a mega-merger to form the biggest corporation of all.

' . . . for AIDS, cancer and autoimmune diseases': another cascade tumbles down towards us, a cascade of info-beings which will cure everything. Without these diseases, health and well-being will join the long list of redundant categories. Being healthy will have either no meaning, or a new meaning, in a world where the old scourges have been defused. Our bodies, like the other objects, will have escaped the old categories through which we have viewed them. Darwin Molecular, like the gene and the ecosystem, is a cyborg packed with worlds waiting to be born.

Across the financial pages, and among our lives, floods an ever-accelerating torrent of new beings. Haraway calls the procession 'hypercapitalist market traffic', and at times the volume of traffic threatens gridlock. Capitalism has gone hyper: faster, weirder, more extravagant, more fictional. This is the real traffic problem facing the new millennium. Hypercapitalism leaves nothing untransformed in its pursuit of growth and profitability. All objects suddenly have the potential to transform without giving us any notice. Tomatoes, rats, human bodies, viruses, cells, databases: objects join hands, they meet, greet and dance together, to the tune of hypercapitalism.

But the earth itself is just another object from this point of view. Why should this object be any different? According to Haraway, in tune with the social theory of Beck, Giddens and Castells, the old earth is passing away, and a new earth is being born. We are witnessing the 'globalisation of the world'. Flavr Savr has been adapted to surpass every local idiosyncrasy; similarly, OncoMouse is on a universal quest. These beings address the whole earth: they are made for that purpose. As the net spreads across, as the old earth becomes the new global system, the hybrid age arrives – the age of which the tomato and the lab rat are symbols, prophets and perhaps fellow-victims.

The market for life is a volatile place. Every being is potentially connected to all the others, and each new link makes its world afresh. Standing further back, Haraway places this global planet in a new 'technoscientific planetary space', orbited not by the moon so much as by communications satellites. If you want to understand what this new planet is like, your best bet is by 'tracing radioisotopes through food chains'.[12] Then you will see just how intricate are the interconnecting networks into which these new entities have fallen. No wonder the financial news of the day is all about mergers. Indeed, to adapt Haraway, just a week before I wrote these words, Time Warner and AOL merged to create the biggest cyborg of them all, the old-new media-Internet company, the traditional avant-garde hybrid, the geek-gened film company, the film-gened book publisher. (Then, as I returned to the text, they both merged with EMI; things have speeded up even since 1994, it seems.)

Inserting a bacterium gene into a tomato is one small change in vegetable marketing; but it is also one large change in the international economy. Flavr Savr and OncoMouse are among the first fully naturalised citizens of the new global earth. They are the rightful inhabitants of 'transnational enterprise culture', which Haraway labels 'the New World Order, Inc'. Nuclear physics was the patron science of the Cold War world; transgenics is the science of this New World Order.[13]

Impurity Hall

Haraway is not celebrating the onset of hypercapitalism. On the contrary, she sees power moving ever further away from the places where most people live. Yet she feels sympathy, even empathy, for the new beings that are born in the wombs of technoscience. The most moving aspect of *Modest_Witness@Second_Millennium* is the affirmation of kinship with all the other non-standard beings. Therefore, if you look through Haraway's eyes, or those of her characters, like OncoMouse and FemaleMan, you will have mixed feelings when you read of Flavr Savr's fate:

> . . . *activists from his Pure Food Campaign would protest the* *tomato . . .*   *The Washington Post,* 21/5/1994

Haraway repeatedly calls herself an 'activist', and she is intuitively sympathetic to all campaigners against the global powers. Yet her work also suggests a reservation about any demand for a return to lost purity. Is Flavr Savr bad because it is impure, her hybrid voices lead one to ask?

This is the troubled heart of the encounter between Donna Haraway and genetic foods, this question of purity and impurity:

> *GM CROPS: GENETIC POLLUTION PROVED*
> Friends of the Earth Press Release,
> www.foe.org.uk, 10.30 p.m., 29/9/1999

The immediate concern was field trials of GM corn, and the 'genetic pollution' referred to the spread of alien pollen. But the phrase 'genetic pollution' also has its other lives, its deeper resonances, whatever the good intentions of those using it. Elsewhere, the Soil Association, voice of organic farming, opposed the same trials on the grounds of 'cross-contamination' (Briefing Paper, June 1999, www.Soilassociation.org), and defended the destruction of GM trial crops; Lord Melchett of Greenpeace referred to 'decontamination'. On the other wing of the argument, we find the 'bio-engineers':

> *BIO-ENGINEERS FIND A WAY TO 'CONTAIN' SUPER* *PLANTS*
> *Researchers at Auburn University have developed a technique*

*that they say should wilt fears that genetically altered plants will
spread their genes around.*

www.CNN.com, 23/4/1998

The dominant voices of *Modest_Witness* are more attuned to
Greenpeace than to Monsanto, and indeed Haraway is sharply
ironic at the expense of a Monsanto-sponsored biology text-
book, seeing in it a crude justification of a vested interest, disguised as science education. And yet, while recognising the
terrifying forces at work in hypercapitalism, Haraway recoils at
the heart of the anti-genetic food arguments, at just that point
where, probably, the arguments have been most persuasive and
influential.

In most protests, the new genetically modified food, and food
crops, appear to be impurities. They are illegitimate hybrids.
Phrases like 'genetic pollution' inevitably come to life in these
arguments. The problem isn't the intentions of the campaigners
or the immediate thrust of the campaigns. The problem is that
this kind of language is haunted. There are ghosts, and perhaps
demons, in the metaphors of endangered purity and genetic contamination. These spirits pay no heed to the aims or meanings
of the campaigners – they are just riding back to life within the
words.

Modest_Witness is always seeking out the viewpoint of the
hybrid, the illicit, the uncategorised being. From that kind of
viewpoint, you hear at work, in the most admirable campaigns,
the old Western demons 'obsessed with racial purity'. Here is
the most difficult act of witnessing. In the name of all the aliens,
the unclean, the uncategorised of the world, Haraway commits
all her many voices to an act of commemoration:

*It is a mistake in this context to forget that anxiety over the
pollution of lineages is at the origin of racist discourse in
European cultures.*

67

Haraway is always intuitively with the activists. Her argument isn't that they are unconsciously racist. But in the language there live the ghosts of other voices, the demons of the old and undead racism of the ages. From the perspective of the cyborgs, the hybrids, such language as 'genetic pollution' can never be innocent of its past, and always risks appealing to the same old reactions, however benign and progressive the immediate intentions.

I cannot help but hear in the biotechnology debates the unintended tones of fear of the alien and suspicion of the mixed.

Haraway's argument is uncompromising, and everything in the book – the way it is written as much as its message – contributes to this moment. You cannot exploit the logic of natural 'kind and purity' at the end of the second millennium without setting foot on haunted ground.

As far as genetics and food goes, then, *Modest_Witness@ Second_Millennium* has a mixed message. This technology is inseparable from hypercapitalism, with its global reach and ambition. But biotechnology is also not identical with this economic system; there is more at work than mere instrumental exploitation. In particular, Haraway wants us to recoil from some of the most influential arguments against genetically modified foods, and crops, and organisms. If you are going to argue against, then you will need to look elsewhere than 'the doctrine of types and intrinsic purposes'. There never was a nature in which all the categories were pure; and it can never be an intrinsic argument against a phenomenon that it involves 'border-crossing' or transgressing categories. If there are things wrong with the new beings, and their sponsors, then it's not their mixed nature that is at fault. Can you really (asks the voice of the witness) believe that, after the 20th century, good will come of arguing against 'implanted alien genes'? Is it really going to be possible to limit the influence of these metaphors to the field in which they are being planted?[14]

Haraway recalls that in 1938, when DuPont first began the

commercial manufacture of nylon, the work was based at a new lab called Purity Hall. It seems, one might elaborate, that the new science of transgenics will be better based at 'Impurity Hall'. This science will breed beings whom others may denounce as 'disharmonious crosses'; it will revel in 'alien genes', which will seem threatening to those who imagine the world used to be pure. Impurity Hall will be as much a centre of capitalism, gone hyper, as Purity Hall was for the earlier phase. This is not a place from which liberation, in any simple sense, will flow among the nations of the world.

Yet there is a positive potential to the science, whatever the dangers involved in its exploitation and ownership. This new 'technoscience' itself will always be a hybrid of pure and applied, commercial and arcane, practice and theory. As the new biology goes about its business of extracting profits, it will also be the agent that 'mixes up all the actors'. In the wake of biological technoscience, the pseudo-scientific basis of 'racial purity' will at last fall into final disrepute. The world will reveal itself, irreversibly, as a place of burgeoning ambiguities. The cause of pure categories may at last be defeated, and the victorious heroes will include 'a bastard mouse', all the cross-patched humans who are its kith and kin, and their endlessly mixed progeny.[15]

Do you feel the world turning upside-down, dear reader? Remember, this supposedly *Modest Witness* is a dangerous character, one who feels drawn to the aliens. Isn't the argument usually the other way round – that the new genetics has sinister links with the old so-called sciences of population control and manipulation, once known as 'eugenics'? Is it not the genetic manipulators who belong to the camp of the race purifiers? Do they not keep alive old dreams of rooting out 'degenerates' by genetic reprogramming? *Modest Witness* testifies against that claim: s/he finds, in the transgenic creatures, allies of all that is unsound, hybrid, anomalous, and, s/he adds, lively and full of the diversity of surprising futures.

Let us have a closer look at this witness . . .

Mutating the Modest Witness

Scientific ideas have always created controversy, both within and beyond science. Nevertheless, looking back as Haraway is doing over the second millennium, science has been a pretty successful way of achieving 'credible witness' in a world where people are bound to disagree about everything they touch. Considering how well-programmed we are to take issue with one another, science has often possessed a truly 'stunning power', none other than the ability 'to establish matters of fact' on many issues, as far as many of its contemporaries have been concerned. In religion and in politics, disagreement rules, and the facts are perpetually in doubt. Facts fuel the arguments between politicians, religious leaders and moral factions. Just listen to a news debate. One side claims that the facts show the economy is improving, and then a torrent of alternative facts pours down on the other side. We find this natural: it is our home, this arguable world. Yet science has been different for the last centuries of the millennium. In those societies where science has become established, people have got used to accepting *scientific* facts as different from ordinary facts. Of course, there is always room to argue about what counts as a science, and there is never a shortage of dissident scientists. But an amazing array of facts has been kept like islands in the rolling oceans of our disputes. These have been facts about all kinds of subjects that we could not possibly check or even question. We have adopted facts about the birth of the universe, or the nature of matter, facts about the origin of species or the development of humanity, facts about the nervous system or the nature of sound.

Science has made facts *believable* in a world of arguments. Haraway tells the story by creating a character called the 'modest witness'. This witness speaks with the scientific voice, and, in the right court, he (for it has been a 'he', predominantly) will be believed, if he issues statements about fact. Haraway is entranced by this lucid authority. The modest witness has seemed to be speaking on behalf of 'the object world'. Everyone else is subjective, and what they say derives from their point of view. But the modest witness is the exception. In his words, we hear the objects speaking, whether they are stones or neurones. The modest witness has been able to ensure 'the clarity and purity of objects'. Thanks to this voice, we know what things are and what they are not.[16]

The new technoscience is different. It challenges the purity of objects. After Flavr Savr, 'tomato' is an ambiguous category, and withdrawing the brand will not alter the effect. The point, of course, is that things always were ambiguous – they overlapped behind our backs, they put out links and held hands when we weren't looking. We have just begun to wake up to the many alliances. Nature no longer stands for purity. But in what voice, then, shall these objects be witnessed? Clearly, the old modest witness will not speak on their behalf.

Take the case of the monarch butterfly. In 1999, research at Cornell University suggested that pollen from modified corn was toxic to the caterpillars of the much-loved monarch butterfly. Friends of the Earth drew this to the attention of President Clinton:

. . . *the alarming new study by scientists at Cornell University . . . find(s) that nearly half of the monarch caterpillars feeding on Bt. corn pollen died after four days . . .*

www.foe.org, 14/6/1999

Of course, facts have always been disputed, even when 'scientists' announced them. But there is something different about these disputes. In Britain, Prince Charles asks whether we really understand these monster crops. In reply, Professor Dereck Burke acerbically comments that:

The well publicised experiments with the Monarch butterfly

71

show that under laboratory conditions caterpillars force-fed corn pollen are damaged . . .

Feedback Magazine, 14/6/1999

There is no distance here between 'the science' and 'the media'. The scientific witness has lost its independence from politics, or religion, where genetic modification is in dispute. No one sees the scientist as an independent witness here; indeed, that is not what this science is for. Here, science has become a dimension of controversy. These claims do not begin as neutral science and then become embroiled in the contentions of politics and religion and ethics. No, these are the claims by which science stirs up the controversies in the first place. In this new world, science and controversy have been spliced as surely as the flounder and the tomato.

But then, where does the book itself speak from? Haraway commits her book early on to a 'contaminated practice'.[17] It would not make sense for *Modest_Witness@Second_Millennium* to speak objectively about the passing of pure objectivity, or neutrally about the obsolescence of scientific neutrality. Haraway's book speaks from an address within the world it interprets. Since that world is impure everywhere you turn, the text can hardly be an island of purity. What is the 'contamination'? In the debates about modified pollen, campaigners refer to the 'contamination' of the environment by alien genes. Haraway's words accept their own contamination. They are nowhere pure. For example, this is a work of social science, drawing upon literatures in anthropology, cultural studies and sociology of science. But it is also a work of fiction, in its format, style and, most important, its thinking. The sentences start out as propositions, turn into metaphorical visions and then uncoil again to yield arguments.

The old-style modest witness aimed to persuade by being, or seeming, transparent. 'These are just the facts; they speak for themselves.' But Haraway is not dealing with a world where such facts occur frequently. They are at least an endangered species. Facts have become contentious claims in arguments in which the status of the parties is precisely the issue. Who does speak for science, anyway?

Haraway's text doesn't just talk about ideas. The words actually seem to come *from* the ideas, they seem able to speak for themselves. For example, Haraway gives an objective-seeming account of OncoMouse, 'the finely-tailored laboratory rodents'. But soon she turns the picture inside-out, declaring that the rodent's 'mutated murine eyes' are the source of her point of view. This text aims to place its sentences inside the perspectives of the ideas and beings it is analysing. These are the moments of affirmation: 'I adopt FemaleMan as my surrogate . . .' Both FemaleMan and OncoMouse live 'after the implosion' in which objectivity and subjectivity, fact and metaphor, collapsed into each other. Haraway is not saying that there are not facts. On the contrary: the book is full of statements which are false if they aren't true, information about biology, about population, about disease and health. But there are not 'pure' facts here; they bring with them contention, they are always within the field of a dispute. If there were no dispute, no one would bother to collect this information and claim it as a fact.

Our guiding text is made in the image of the creatures it is interpreting: the moth-proofed potato, the cancer-prone rat, the super-squash. Would you trust a guide to such a weird world if s/he sounded familiar and straightforward? There are moments when the author, or her voice, seems to be taken over by the world. Looking inwards, Haraway the writer finds strange births happening in her own words: 'Narrative timescapes proliferate in the flesh of my sentences . . . '; the past is spliced to the future, the story of progress to the parable of disaster.[18]

The crucial question is this: who are we to trust in the new world? This question reaches far beyond genetic food to a host of environmental issues, health crises and risks. We are in a phase where *trust* itself is the main subject at issue. The disputes about genetic food are strong examples of this more general trend. The problem is to decide what kind of voice to believe. Haraway is not telling you what to believe. But she is suggesting that you re-think what kind of witness you trust.

The FemaleMan and OncoMouse are, finally, modest witnesses to world-changing matters of fact . . .

You had better start trusting the ambiguous ones, the voices which cannot be defined. If you want to understand these new facts, then try imagining them from the perspective of the cancer-prone saviour rat. Seek out the most ambiguous viewpoint, and re-view the facts from there. In effect, Haraway is claiming that the new genetic facts are not just more information. They represent a change in the whole nature of information. Facts are not what they used to be. These ideas, of course, are themselves ambiguous! But one of the things they mean is that these facts are spliced with all kinds of uncertainties. These are not facts that are cut and dried. They include possibilities, a whole calculus of what might and might not happen.

Let's recall Flavr Savr, and GM corn, and moth potato. Put the question to them: are you safe? The answer takes the form of statements about probability, including the probabilities of harm from other foods, like 'normal' burgers or chips or chocolate. In addition, the facts about genetic foods are saturated facts; they are suffused by theories. You can't separate the basic information about Flavr Savr from complex theories about DNA or about evolution itself. Haraway calls such data 'world-changing matters of fact': these are facts within certain worlds.[19] In other words, to accept the 'fact' that a squash is now 'naturally' resistant to decay involves entering a certain world, and leaving another one behind. In that new world, there are new facts. But if you stay in the old world, these will not look like the 'facts'. This doesn't mean that someone isn't right, someone else wrong. But it means that we will need new ways of deciding.

Haraway is writing with a purpose, call it even a moral purpose, in the sense that novelists can have a moral purpose: 'I want a mutated modest witness . . .' The old modest witnesses were plausible experts. They spoke objectively about experiments which yielded clear results. They referred their arguments to scientific theories which were accepted by strong expert communities. Somewhere at the end of the second millennium, we stopped trusting those old witnesses. The cynical explanation is that they gave one too many reassurances that turned out false, or warnings that turned out unnecessary. We gave up butter, only to find ourselves recommended it again. We were told that British beef was safe to eat, and then the roof fell in. But Haraway has a deeper explanation. The facts have become more complicated. They have changed their nature. A fact about Flavr Savr is just not the same kind of thing as a fact about oak trees, or rubber, or the moon. It has more in common with facts about, say, Black Holes, or programming 'languages'. These are 'mutated' facts – full of theories, full of uncertainties and ambiguities. You have to grasp these new facts as much with your imagination as with your calculator.

Mutant Universities

A scientific article about genes and food is a form of knowledge, or would-be knowledge; so, in a different way, is a newspaper article. But the Flavr Savr is also a form of knowledge, and not just any other being in the world. Similarly, a book about cancer aims to be accepted as knowledge. A news item aims to spread, or question, that knowledge. But OncoMouse is also a form of knowledge, as well as a means of gaining further information. Knowledge can take the form of words, or of objects, and even, now, of living beings.

Universities try to produce knowledge, much of it in the form of texts. But they also produce the new living knowledge, the information-organisms. Let us summon OncoMouse again, this time to bear witness to the nature of her creator.

MUTANT MICE IN EUROPEAN TEST CASE
Mutant mice bred by Harvard University turned into a test case . . .

AP, 21/1/1993

This item is about the European legal battle to secure a patent for OncoMouse for its original inventors, Harvard University. The university, as we have seen, already held the patent in the US:

Its US patent was granted in 1988, the first ever for an artificially engineered natural life form.

The creature seems to be alarming because it breaks all the boundaries: artificial and natural, engineered and living. But the news report also emphasises that its ownership is equally hybrid:

DuPont de Nemours and Bio, Inc. of Wilmington, Delaware own the commercial rights.

The mouse is an academic product and a commercial commodity; it is a research tool and a space in a sales catalogue; it is the hope of a cure and the gleam of a profit. All the categories are in flux together, and among them is the university itself. In making OncoMouse, Harvard also re-made itself. OncoMouse, by its presence, testifies to something fundamental about Harvard and its kin: they too have a new family system.

If knowledge is changing, then you would expect the institutions of learning and research to change too. Harvard is spliced with DuPont, the company we saw earlier at the heart of the plastics revolution and then the atomic age. This splicing is the inevitable complement to the new genetic inventions. Spliced institutions create the hybrid world within which such inventions occur. OncoMouse's natural habitat is this place where Harvard and DuPont merge. Other genetic innovations will inhabit an even more ambiguous world:

The Cambridge Massachusetts-based Millennium researchers, collaborating with Switzerland-based Hoffman-La Roche as well as other pharmaceutical labs and academic centers, have been seeking the receptor gene . . .

AP, 29/12/1995

You can no longer say where the academic centres stop and the commercial organisations start; nor can you be sure where the USA stops and Switzerland starts. More subtly, you can't be sure where pharmaceutics stops and genetics starts. The university used to be a system of well-patrolled borders – between disciplines, and between the academy and various outside worlds. True, there were many secret crossings; but now that there is a new age, the border controls have been removed. Instead, from these 'academic centres' flies a flag with the motto: Welcome to the hybrid world!

In the previous section, we saw Haraway exploring the ambiguities of her own writing, and of communication in general. She is equally interested in these institutions, or networks, where knowledge is created. She traces, for example, the interlinkage of Harvard and DuPont back to the late 1970s in the biotech field, and sees the connection as 'a trademark of the symbiosis between industry and academia'.[20] Trademarks belong to the economic world; symbiosis is part of nature. Again, the categories curve into each other. So, again, the 'basic technique of gene splicing' is covered by a spliced patent, the Stanley-Cohen-Herbert-Boyer Patent. The ownership passes across two universities, Stanford and the University of California at San Francisco, and there are added industrial interests.

Haraway is trying to show the logic of a world in action. Here, nothing stays distinct and separate. To exist is to have a potential for becoming connected to other entities, for being absorbed or overlapped or redefined. The university is no different from the tomato in this respect: it has no clear boundaries, but exists in relation with other entities. There is no firm inside and outside to the university, any more than there is to the squash.

Haraway can see only too clearly how these overlaps and mergers could look like another kind of corruption. Are we not losing our institutes of 'pure' learning? Kin of OncoMouse, admirer of deviant flounders, Haraway has no time for this melancholy. She denounces 'nostalgia for "pure research"' on several grounds. For one thing, knowledge never was pure, it only tried to appear pure. For another thing, the hybrid mentality is fundamentally creative. She refers, for example, to 'the complex splice between computer science and molecular biology', a splice out of which the new genetics has evolved. True, there is plenty to worry about in the 'corporatization of biology', which is a less happy way to describe the 'symbiosis' of university and industry. The serious danger is the threat to 'social criticism'. Will universities that depend on these huge partnerships still be home to critics of the same economic system? It is not purity that is the loss, but criticism, itself a mixed-up hybrid activity, part intellect and part emotion, part detachment and part involvement.[21]

The book's address specifies a time: *@Second_Millennium*. The turn of the millennium is itself a hybrid time, where eras are spliced together, and where memory and prophecy intermingle. In that moment, the university also mutates, and Haraway with it, for she is writing from one such mutant. With shades of disgust, of anger and of hope, she seeks to bear witness within this changed institution, and that is one of the main reasons why she has taken so much care over the genetic new wave. For these product-beings carry within themselves the pattern of our institutes of learning: spliced, incongruous and potentially creative.

We tend to think of knowledge as being part of the search to discover the truth about our world. But for Haraway the new knowledge is made of 'world-making practices'. That is, knowledge now seizes upon the world and re-makes it. In the 18th century, the first botanical scientists classified the plants; at the turn of the millennium, their hybrid descendants are re-mixing the categories. You could say new connections are being revealed, or that new links are being made, or that the true boundaries are being destroyed. Is nature yielding her true secrets, when the flounder comes to the rescue of the decaying tomato? In Haraway's terms, the answer is 'yes and no': we are helping to reshape nature, from within, at the same time as we seek understanding.

Haraway adopts the principle that 'Nothing comes without its world'. In the case of Flavr Savr, or genetically modified soybean, that world includes the mutant universities of the second millennium. Does the world create these beings, or do they create that world? There is no clear answer. Without the new world, there are no new beings, and without the new beings, there is no new world. Haraway talks, ambiguously, of 'forging knowledges': who can say any longer exactly when knowledge is genuine? Throughout the Cold War, social theorists talked of the 'military-industrial complex'. Now, Haraway suggests, we can also talk of the academic-industrial complex, a huge system that forges new knowledge in hundreds of brilliant new ways. We live in the age of the knowledge forgers, and they are the ones who have sent as their 'vanguard' Flavr Savr and GM corn and OncoMouse.[22]

The Transgenic Millennium

We began with the question of whether the world would soon be seeing the last of the genetic foods. Haraway explains why these beings are not going to leave us alone. The vegetable mutants aren't going to get back into their space capsules and head for home. The reason isn't so much to do with the economics of food marketing, or consumer demand, or the supermarket retail system, or attitudes towards health and risk. All of those factors have a short-term influence. But, *Modest_Witness @Second_Millennium* shows, these foods and food-crops represent a new age, an age with many other embodiments, from 'databases' to universities, from custom-built rats to biological computer chips. Yes, it is the age of 'hypercapitalism', the time when, as the social theorist Anthony Giddens puts it, we feel ourselves living in 'a runaway world'.[23] But there is also immense creativity at work. Sometimes, this sounds like mere political cliché-mongering – Cool Britannia and all that nonsense. But Haraway shows that there is something more genuinely liberating going on. And, on the other side, there are some sinister aspects to the recoil from poor old flounderised tomatoes.

Haraway isn't trying to persuade us to buy genetic. Actually, the book leaves us to our own uncertainties as consumers. But she is warning us not to settle for some of the anti-genetic rhetoric, and also to acknowledge to ourselves the degree to which our world is changing. We need to re-tool *all* our reasons, for and against weird new foods, and for and against all kinds of other beings and concepts. At the heart of *Modest_Witness*, there is a vision of 'the time'. It is that vision which I now wish to explore, as we move towards Haraway's anti-conclusion, her refusal to settle into a fixed response or verdict.

Throughout *Modest_Witness*, one of the organising concepts is the 'chronotope': the phenomenon which represents its time. Literally, a 'chronotope' defines what is 'topical' in a period. These are the images and ideas, the objects and events in which the age finds its meanings. For Haraway, the central chronotopes of the present age are 'the gene and the computer'.[24] They are more than mere symbols, these presences – they are the means by which we organise our sense of ourselves in history. The gene and the computer are our ways of defining what makes our time different from those that went before. It is, of course, quite right to have mixed reactions to the computer and all of its associated phenomena. Haraway isn't saying that just because something is a chronotope, we have to worship it, or even like it. But it would be a mistake to think you can just get it out of your life.

One way to tell whether something is a chronotope is to try to have no view of it at all. If it really is one of the time's defining topics, you will probably find that you have a surplus of views about it, some hostile, some welcoming. Even trying to ignore the gene and the computer becomes an expression of a fundamental attitude. What you think about the gene is more than just another of your ideas and values. These are core values; they have consequences everywhere else in your life. You can easily see why the computer is a defining subject. Just remember all that anxiety about the millennium bug, how many aspects of everyday life suddenly seemed hooked up to the computer. The gene is also diffused through everyday life – after Flavr Savr, all food really *is* 'genetic food', modified or apparently unmodified. The gene stands for *your* chances of getting diseases, and gene therapy for *your* hope of avoiding them. The gene is the secret language of life chances. In our reactions to genetic foods, we are starting to explore our hopes and fears for the whole genetic age.

When genes first became a moral issue, they were all about purity: how good are your genes, how pure is your pedigree? Now the gene is all about crossing-over. What plutonium did for the elements, transgenic organisms will do for the organic realm, the species. Both the transuranic elements and the transgenic organisms are:

Earthshaking artificial productions . . . whose status as aliens on earth, and indeed in the entire solar system, has changed who we are fundamentally and permanently . . . [25]

There is a famous poem by the American poet Wallace Stevens, called 'Anecdote of a Jar', in which an entire landscape folds itself around one small man-made object. For Haraway, the equivalent poem would be 'Anecdote of a Gene', say the flounder gene in one tomato or the bacterial gene in its fellow. In the Stevens poem, a vast panorama of mountains comes into new form in the presence of the jar. In Haraway's poem, the panorama of the solar system itself takes a new shape in the presence of these 'trans' genes.

How can the migratory gene be so significant? In the presence of these mobile genes, we can no longer talk with confidence about 'nature' or 'culture'. When an article claims that a modified vegetable will 'naturally' resist disease, that is a small sign that the category of 'nature' no longer exists. It has been replaced by a hybrid for which as yet there is no new name. But 'nature' and 'culture' are not just any old categories: they are connected to almost all of the big ideas through which we define and evaluate ourselves and our lives. We think of our own characteristics as partly given by nature, and partly acquired through participation in culture. Huge debates have raged, over the last four hundred years, over how far 'nature' makes us what we are, how far we are products of 'nurture'. You can see these arguments arising in Shakespeare, and you can find their direct descendants in current dilemmas about education and social policy. But every time we look at the world, we use the concepts of nature and culture to orient our gaze. That over there is a natural object – the sky, say, or those clouds. On the horizon, those shapes are man-made – the line of rooftops or the flag flying. We have become adept at scanning the world for nature and culture, and we negotiate all kinds of ambiguities with every glance. That flower bed is cultivated nature. But we also look at actions as natural or cultural. It is natural, say, to want a home; it is cultural to want plaster ducks on the wall. No more: after the migration of the gene, we are going to have to begin to unlearn these habits, if Haraway is right.

In fact, she believes that for a long time the division has been illusory. But now the illusion is being shattered by a cascade of new objects under our noses, and in our mouths: 'Potent categories collapse into each other.'[26] In Haraway's view, Western culture is in a moment of really profound transfiguration. This is the meaning that she reads into her encounter with the monster tomatoes and other genetically new beings.

All cultures depend upon categories. They are ways of dividing up the world, and indeed we have no chance to construct a world at all without these divisions, for we would be facing only a flux of shadows. Recent work in anthropology, such as George Lakoff's *Women, Fire and Dangerous Things*, has explored the central role of categories in the formation of cultures: nature and culture, fire and water, earth and air, body and spirit, male and female, all play their part. But, as Lakoff shows, categories are never nice neat boxes; they are bundles of fizzing potential for thought and experience.[27] Haraway, as a feminist, has been concerned to analyse the failings of inherited categories, and the potential for new ones. Now, in the moment of OncoMouse and FemaleMan, she senses a change which affects all the categories in Western thought. We are leaving the era when it even seemed plausible to treat our categories, like nature and culture, male and female, as fixed and bounded entities. A category never was so clear-cut in any event. But now, at the second millennium, we are witnessing the birth of the hybrid categories. The divisions will never again even *seem* fixed. We are going to have to learn to live, think and even experience afresh.

To see just how deep the change is, we can turn from Haraway back to the birth of the category in Western thought, in Aristotle's book *The Categories*.[28] There, in the 4th century BC, Aristotle is trying to define what it means for two things to share a 'name'. He gives as his first example an anomaly: 'For instance, while a man and a portrait can properly both be called "animals", these are equivocally named.' What he means is that the category of 'animals' is not being employed in the same way if you use it for both a living man and his portrait. By contrast, the situation is no longer equivocal when you say that 'a man and an ox are called "animals"'. Then the category is uniform and unambiguous. So the first example of a category is 'animal', and the first problem that arises is precisely on the borders where nature and culture meet and are distinguished. For Aristotle, 'animal' is the prototype category. If you can't tell what you mean by 'animal' and 'not-animal', then you don't belong to his world. But what about the gene which migrates from that giant moth to the potato? It doesn't turn the vegetable *into* an animal, true, but in Haraway's terms it collapses both categories. We have to rethink what we mean when we classify things and beings.

Aristotle gives a second example. This time he wants to explain where categories stop. His term for a category here is 'genus', used in modern biology still, and he is very much pre-occupied with the biological realm:

Take the genera, for example, animal and knowledge. 'Footed', 'two-footed', 'winged', 'aquatic' are among the differentiae of animal. But none will be found to distinguish a particular species of knowledge. No species of knowledge will differ from another in being 'two-footed'.

Let us pursue the dialogue. Haraway replies on behalf of the new millennium:

. . . the organism for us is an information system of a different kind . . . [29]

This is the inner significance of the postmodern encounter between Donna Haraway and Flavr Savr or OncoMouse, and, by implication, between ourselves and mutated soybeans. We don't need to love them, or even buy them. But we need, Haraway argues, to bear witness to their meaning, to the world that they signify, a world in which both they and we might be fellow-victims or fellow-inheritors. Knowledge and animal are now overlapping categories, and in that moment all the rest of the old 'genera' will overlap in their turn. The new millennium is transgenic.

Beyond Goodies and Baddies

Is there a moral to this postmodern encounter between Donna Haraway and genetic foods? One moral is clearly missing. You cannot go to Haraway in order to find the answer to the question: is genetic food safe or unsafe? You won't leave *Modest_Witness* newly decisive about your next shopping trip. Nor will you be clearer about your views the next time you read a news item about GM technology. You won't be more confident in your outrage against Monsanto, or more definitive about Greenpeace and their tactics. But I think it would be a good thing if Haraway's ideas were more widely known, and that they would benefit the entire discussion of genetic issues, including the food controversies.

The question of what Haraway offers is inseparable from the larger issue of what such thinkers are for. What do we want from our cultural theorists and philosophers, our science historians and political analysts? What, in other words, do we want from those thinkers who deal with social, cultural and ethical topics? Do we want them to remove ambiguities, to produce a simpler world, to make the best decisions clear? Do we want thinkers to show us whether to vote for New Labour? Do we want thinkers who will decide for us whether the Internet is good or bad for us and our children? Do you want to read ideas that will leave you more certain than before – one less dilemma, one more decision? There are plenty of candidates for such a role. The shelves are full of authoritative advice and definitive prediction. Is it not the responsibility of experts to provide answers?

Haraway has a different conception of the thinker's responsibility. Her work is certainly not neutral, and she takes sides on many questions. Yet the whole effect isn't to reduce the ambiguity of the world. Instead, we leave Haraway with a more focused sense of the real ambiguity of things, an ambiguity which will have to be part of any answers that we choose to give, any commitments we make. In Haraway's approach, ambiguity and commitment go together. That is what 'grown-up' commitment is all about: recognising the ambiguities of the world, including of one's own positions.

In another context, Haraway has been a strong admirer of the work of the French philosopher, novelist and feminist Simone de Beauvoir. I suggest that Beauvoir's book *The Ethics of Ambiguity* (1947) offers a good perspective on the value of Haraway's own thinking for us, as we turn back to the confusing world of genetic controversies. For Beauvoir, writing in the immediate aftermath of the Second World War, it would be the height of irresponsibility for a serious thinker to try to make the world seem less ambiguous. Such an approach would even, in her view, diminish the humanity of all involved:

To attain his truth, man must not attempt to dispel the ambiguity of his being, but, on the contrary, to accept the task of realising it.[30]

In *The Second Sex* (1949), Beauvoir reassessed this idiom of 'man', an enterprise that Haraway continues in her treatment of 'FemaleMan'. Meanwhile, coiled within the sentence, lies a rich concept of 'the ambiguity of . . . being'. In this approach, the task of the thinker is to help people realise the full ambiguity of their own being, and of the world to which that being bears witness. No one could accuse Beauvoir of being uncommitted: she stands as a model for the modern committed thinker. But her commitment includes this embracing of ambiguity.

In the largest perspective, I believe Haraway's approach to genetic controversy carries on Beauvoir's 'ethic of ambiguity'. Every phrase of Haraway's argument presses forward in a definite direction but with a continuing sense of ambiguity.

This implosion issuing in a wonderful bestiary of cyborgs . . .

You can feel the danger of the moment, and at the same time the excitement of a changing horizon. There can be no new possibilities which are entirely pure, not issuing from our world. These new beings are ambiguous because we ourselves put the ambiguity into them in the first place. To evade the ambiguity of 'these genetically strange inflected proprietary beings' is to run away from your own ambiguity.[31] Like Beauvoir, Haraway seeks a grown-up commitment.

The philosopher Nietzsche called one of his late works *Beyond Good and Evil*. There he demanded that we recognise 'man's comprehensiveness and multiplicity'.[32] After Beauvoir and with Haraway, perhaps we can begin to make our own commitments in a world beyond goodies and baddies, where the issues will not take our decisions for us.

When you turn back to the continuing debate about genetic foods, I think you can see why this ethic of ambiguity could be so important. On one side, you have the goodies riding to the defence of progress:

Renowned US scientists James Watson and Norman Borlaug join more than 1,000 other scientists from around the world in endorsing the 'Declaration of Scientists in Support of Agricultural Biotechnology' . . .

Business World, 21/2/2000

And in case you missed the point, you are told just who is who: 'Norman Borlaug, who is considered the "Father of the Green Revolution" . . .'! But then on the other side, you have the goodies too, the brave and outgunned seadogs defending the English coast from an invading foreigner:

Environmental activists have ambushed a ship loaded with genetically modified soya and vowed to stay on board until the cargo was returned to the United States . . .

www.ITN.co.uk, 25/2/2000

Such heroic figures seem to offer an escape, in opposite directions, from the ambiguity of being. But to embrace ambiguity does not mean to tread a nice, clear 'third way'. In fact, there is nothing ambiguous about the rhetoric of the middle ground on genetic foods, as on other issues. Here is British Prime Minister Tony Blair trying to recognise ambiguity and be right all the way:

'The potential for good highlights why we were right not to slam the door on GM food or crops without further research. The potential for harm shows why we are right to proceed very cautiously indeed.'

www.ITN.co.uk, 27/2/2000

On one side there is rightness, and the same on the other. This is the very reverse of an ethic of ambiguity.

By contrast, Haraway offers a space where we can recognise the 'wholeness and multiplicity' of these strange new beings, a multiplicity which is, in many ways, a reflection of our own creative energies coming back to greet us. Above all, we can acknowledge our kinship with these new possibilities, either as victims or as heroes. What lies beyond the goodies and baddies, beyond the old categories? Does the idea of utopia itself survive beyond the old definitions? In the light of this postmodern encounter, I suggest that any ideal future would be one which could embrace ambiguity, rather than cure or redefine it. Haraway names such a prospect 'heterogeneous well-being', a fulfilment of ambiguity rather than an escape back into definition.[33]

Notes

1. Haraway's most famous single work is 'A Cyborg Manifesto', originally published in 1985 and variously reprinted, including in her own collection, *Simians, Cyborgs, and Women* (London: Free Association Books, 1991). Here she takes a feminist leap into the realm of science fiction futures. Additional information on Haraway's works is given in the section on Further Reading.

2. Donna J. Haraway, *Modest_Witness@Second_Millennium. Female Man©_Meets_OncoMouse™* (New York and London: Routledge, 1997), p. 62.

3. Ibid., p. 88.

4. The genes of this tomato and its suspect kin are identified on pp. 59–60 of *Modest_Witness*.

5. The transuranic elements and the new genetics are set in context on pp. 51–6 of *Modest_Witness*.

6. Ibid., p. 85.

7. Ibid., p. 57.

8. Ibid., p. 60, where Haraway makes her confession of style.

9. Ibid., pp. 88–9, on the revolution in kinship.

10. Haraway's declaration on behalf of her cyborgs is made on p. 12 of *Modest_Witness*, except for the definition of Machine and Human, from p. 59.

11. The vivid response to the appearance of OncoMouse™ is given on p. 79 of *Modest_Witness*, except for the definition of Machine and Human, from p. 59.

12. The treatment of hypercapital and the globe appears on pp. 12–14 of *Modest_Witness*.

13. Ibid., p. 54.

14. The impassioned critique of racist reverberation is carried forward on pp. 60–2 of *Modest_Witness*.

15. The theme of purity echoes across *Modest_Witness*, as these quotes show. Purity Hall is identified on p. 86, the alien genes are from p. 62, and the idea of a genetic re-mix is on p. 121.

16. The history and critique of 'modest witnessing' is on pp. 22–4 of *Modest_Witness*.

17. Ibid., p. 8.

18. The discussion of perspective evolves through *Modest_Witness*

from p. 52 on the rodent viewpoint, to p. 70 on FemaleMan and p. 84 on narrative itself. The twisting form of this discussion helps to convey the essential idea.

19. Ibid., p. 121.

20. Ibid., p. 80.

21. The analysis of the new research institutes is carried out on pp. 90–7 of *Modest_Witness*.

22. The analysis of worlds and their knowledge is on p. 37 of *Modest_Witness*.

23. Anthony Giddens, *The Runaway World* (London: Profile, 1999).

24. The 'chronotope' is introduced on pp. 41–2 of *Modest_Witness*.

25. Ibid., p. 55.

26. Ibid., p. 68.

27. George Lakoff, *Women, Fire and Dangerous Things: What Categories Reveal About The Mind* (Chicago: University of Chicago Press, 1987).

28. Aristotle, *The Categories*, translated by H. P. Cooke (Cambridge, Mass.: Harvard University Press, 1938). The examples are taken from Book I.

29. *Modest_Witness*, p. 97.

30. Simone de Beauvoir, *The Ethics of Ambiguity*, translated by B. Frechtman (New York: Capitol Press, 1996), p. 13.

31. The vision of the imploding bestiary is on p. 43 of *Modest_Witness*.

32. The quotation is from the translation in *The Portable Nietzsche*, edited and translated by W. Kaufmann (New York: Penguin, 1954), p. 445.

33. The assertion of a new well-being is made on p. 95 of *Modest_Witness*.

Further Reading

I hope this discussion might encourage readers to make their own way into the major work in question, Donna J. Haraway, *Modest_Witness@ Second_Millennium. FemaleMan©_Meets_OncoMouse™* (New York and London: Routledge, 1997). The central section for the current topic is Part II.2, 'FemaleMan©_Meets_OncoMouse™'. This covers the cyborg, transgenetic organisms, FemaleMan and OncoMouse, all from the perspective of border-crossings and ambiguities. The richest linkages then run forward to Part III.6, 'Race: Universal Donors in a Vampire Culture' (pp. 213–66), where the full moral and political consequences of the argument are unfolded.

Haraway's thinking always generates fertile interconnections. From *Modest_Witness*, these reach back most richly to her collection entitled *Simians, Cyborgs, and Women* (London: Free Association Books, 1991), where the reader can find one version of the famous essay on cyborgs, under the title 'A Cyborg Manifesto: Science, Technology and Socialist-Feminism in the Late Twentieth Century'. This can also be found in Linda J. Nicholson (ed.), *Feminism/Postmodernism* (New York and London: Routledge, 1990), as 'A Manifesto For Cyborgs'. The first version appeared in *Socialist Review*, 15.80 (1985). There is a rich array of responses and dialogues in Chris Hables Gray (ed.), *The Cyborg Handbook* (New York and London: Routledge, 1995), from which N. Katherine Hayles, 'The Life Cycle of Cyborgs', is especially relevant. Haraway's own *Cyborg Babies* (New York and London: Routledge, 1998) follows the question of technoscience into a different moral terrain.

Finally, *Modest_Witness* belongs with a group of distinguished works which have attempted to comprehend the new relationships between science, technology and culture. The most relevant are:

Ulrich Beck, *World Risk Society* (Cambridge: Polity Press, 1999).
Manuel Castells, *End of Millennium* (Malden, Mass. and Oxford: Blackwell, 1997).
Bruno Latour, *Pandora's Hope* (Cambridge, Mass. and London: Harvard University Press, 1999).

Plato and
the Internet

Kieron O'Hara

The Knowledge Economy

We are now living, we are often told, in a knowledge economy. In the past, the key to wealth was a plentiful supply of labour and control of natural resources. Nowadays, though, developments in technology – particularly computer and telecommunications technology – have resulted in undreamt-of ease in transferring data around the world. A scientific paper written yesterday in New York can be running off the printers today in researchers' offices in San Francisco, London, Sydney, Tokyo or Beijing. Scientists can collaborate without ever meeting face to face. Desktop computers can alert their operators to the latest news items, stock prices or cricket scores as they change.

In this new world, the important source of competitive advantage for a developed economy is no longer raw materials or labour, but *knowledge:* bright ideas, smart designs, clever organisation. It can't compete in brawn, so it must use brain. The new economy demands *knowledge workers* who create value and wealth, not with traditional money capital, but with *intellectual capital.*[1] Indeed, many hold out the hope that the exploitation of knowledge could be a key to enriching the developing world too, in that knowledge capital is easier to find and cheaper to get hold of than money capital, and the World Bank's Global Development Network has been set up to explore that possibility.[2]

All this is independent of the dotcom boom and bust. Knowledge is big business in any industry. A huge amount is invested annually in knowledge via research and development programmes, staff training, and so on; but because knowledge is intangible, it can't be measured or accounted for. As consultant Alan Burton-Jones puts it, 'Knowledge is transforming the nature of production and thus work, jobs, the firm, the market, and every aspect of economic activity. Yet knowledge is currently a poorly understood and thus undervalued economic resource.'[3]

What is Knowledge? The Discipline of Epistemology

So it makes sense, in this new world, to get to know about knowledge itself: what it is, how you spot it, how you make sure you have enough of it. It turns out that there are people who investigate these issues – the study of knowledge is a branch of philosophy called *epistemology*. Epistemologists investigate such questions as: What is knowledge? Are there different types of knowledge? Are there procedures that you can follow to make sure you acquire knowledge? How do you know that something *is* knowledge? How do you discover whether you are mistaken? Can you know what you don't know?

Epistemology is not the oldest branch of philosophy, but damn near. The first philosopher whose epistemological work has come down to us in any quantity is Plato (*c.* 428–*c.* 347 BC). Such was the power of his influence on later philosophers that much epistemology since has continued along more or less the same lines. Indeed, even in the present day, epistemologists are wrestling with problems (and providing answers) that bear a strong resemblance to Plato's.

In this twenty-first-century context, there are many dilemmas that Plato would recognise. For instance, how do we sort out the knowledge from the dross on the World Wide Web, the true from the false? Even so, can it be right that epistemology should still operate from essentially Ancient Greek assumptions? Does the emergence of massive and thoroughgoing technological change make *no* difference to the epistemological landscape? Or alternatively, do we need to look afresh at the phenomenon of knowledge in the Internet age?

This is the question I will examine in this book. I will sketch the traditional philosophical arguments, to give a rough idea of the general Platonic position that still holds sway today. Then I'll talk about the technological, commercial and political context which has made the study of knowledge suddenly so pressing. To close, I'll bring the ideas of traditional epistemology together with the new technology, to see how far, if at all, the discipline has to change.

Scepticism

In order to understand the historical roots of modern epistemology, let us begin by asking why Plato studied knowledge in the first place. Plato's opponents in his writings on knowledge were philosophers who were *sceptical* about knowledge, who didn't believe, for some reason, that it was possible to gain knowledge at all.

Such sceptics[4] included the *Sophists* of the fifth century BC, fiercely critical philosophers who tried to explain the universe in terms of the way it appears, rather than by making up theories about what underlies its appearance. Unfortunately, by attracting the ire not only of Plato but Aristotle as well, they garnered a reputation as bloody-minded quibblers more concerned with showing their verbal dexterity than finding the truth, keen to show wrong right and right wrong. They, no doubt, saw themselves as *anti-theorists*, undermining spurious attempts to divine the occult phenomena that supposedly lay behind experience. They were much more interested in the use of argument for practical purposes (e.g., in the law-courts, or in the lively Athenian democracy), rather than for 'pure' metaphysical speculation.

Be that as it may, the Sophists' attack on theories, and on the practical deployment of argument, made them very potent and worthy of Plato's opposition. There is a lot of power in a theory – think of the status of science and scientists today. In general, sceptics do not try to argue on the theorists' terms (like one scientist arguing that another's experiment was poorly designed in some way), but instead try to suggest that the whole theory itself is unfounded. Nowadays, a space-age Sophist would probably say that if you download a page from the World Wide Web, you might as well take it at face value because there's no way you can reliably find out whether it's true or false. It's an anti-authoritarian gesture; it says that all these expensive scientists and journalists and commentators have no special access to truth. And it has a surface plausibility, in that it is very difficult to ground a theory securely on unimpeachable foundations. If you keep asking 'But how do you know *that*?', eventually you will get the testy answer, 'I just *do*, that's all!' And when the expensive establishment thinkers get it wrong – in Plato's day, with the decline of Athenian power; in recent times, with the BSE crisis – there is further circumstantial evidence against rooted knowledge/power structures.

In general, scepticism is found attractive as a doctrine by thinkers who worry about glib answers to deep questions, and as a rhetorical device (a stiff test) by those who would hope their theories stand up to the most rigorous scrutiny. Ancient sceptics included Pyrrho, Sextus Empiricus and Cicero; in more modern times scepticism has been used by thinkers as diverse as Montaigne and Descartes, Hume and Hayek. Little wonder that Plato, theorist extraordinaire, deeply opposed the sceptical strain of thought and devoted such a large amount of time to trying to refute it.

Plato and Knowledge: The Birth of Epistemology

Even though we have much of Plato's writing, and even though Plato is a very lucid writer, the actual substance of his thought is not as clear as it might be.[5] For one thing, rather than producing work in the standard form of a treatise or monograph, in which the author sets forward his own view and defends it against counter-argument, Plato wrote *dialogues*. Such dialogues were generally led by Socrates, for whom Plato had great affection,[6] and included other prominent philosophers, Sophists and public figures of the day (typically, the dialogue would be named after one of the participants – Theaetetus, Meno, Gorgias, etc.).

Plato – who does not appear – usually, but not always, can be taken as endorsing the views expressed by Socrates. But the dialogues are rarely conclusive, and at the end the participants often agree to differ. In the *Parmenides*, Socrates puts forward arguments that we can confidently attribute to Plato, yet is overwhelmed by Parmenides' criticisms, and the reader is left in little doubt that Parmenides is the moral victor in that one.

Plato's philosophy was not an ivory-tower pursuit without application to the real world. His home city of Athens had recently suffered a terrible reverse in war, amid scandal, corruption and military and naval incompetence. He believed that a properly run city needed a trained class of rulers. Athenian boys were taught how to wrestle or swim; why could they not be taught the virtues appropriate for a good leader? This is a riddle which has always intrigued humanity; indeed, the English public-school system was one attempt at an answer.

As Plato observed, there are great disputes over the nature of virtue. But if we don't know what virtue *is* – and these disputes imply that we don't – how can we teach it? Many of the early dialogues consist in Socrates demonstrating that his interlocutors do not really *know* what virtue is, and so the question of knowledge – what knowledge of virtue, or anything else for that matter, consists in – loomed large in Plato's work. His ideas changed somewhat over his career, and I don't want to go into the particular details of his epistemological views in this book. But the main point is that he drew an interesting and compelling distinction between *knowledge* and *true belief*.

SOCRATES: *Do you think that knowing and believing are the same, or is there a difference between knowledge and belief?*
GORGIAS: *I should say that there is a difference.*
SOCRATES: *Quite right; and you can prove it like this. If you were asked whether there are such things as true and false beliefs, you would say that there are, no doubt.*
GORGIAS: *Yes.*

SOCRATES: *But are there such things as true or false knowledge?*
GORGIAS: *Certainly not.*
SOCRATES: *Then knowledge and belief are clearly not the same thing.*

(*Gorgias*, 454cd)[7]

True beliefs are useful, and will not lead you astray. But they are not reliable, in that you could never be sure about them.

SOCRATES: *True opinions are a fine thing, and do all sorts of good so long as they stay in their place; but they will not stay long. They run away from a man's mind, so they are not worth much until you tether them by working out the reason* [why they are true].

(*Meno*, 97e–98a)

Plato spent much effort trying to establish the essential difference between knowledge and true belief, particularly in his great epistemological work, the *Theaetetus*. In that work, Socrates and Theaetetus spend a large part of the middle section comparing knowledge and true belief (187b–201c). The close of the dialogue discusses a theory that knowledge is true belief plus something called a *logos* (201c–210b).

The nature of this *logos* has proved troublesome for philosophers to interpret[8] – it seems to be a sort of explanation or rational account – and anyway Plato does not seem enthused by the idea. The dialogue comes out against the 'knowledge = belief + *logos*' theory. Nevertheless, these discussions and suggestions have been very influential in later philosophy. Knowledge has a reliability that true belief doesn't; to have confidence in your true beliefs, you must give some sort of justification of them. This justification process, whatever it may be, is what turns a belief into knowledge; it makes it *reliable*.

Let us call this analysis of knowledge as 'justified true belief' the 'JTB analysis'.

Other Types of Knowledge

But is all knowledge like this? Using the idea of a belief that happens to be true to point up the essential reliability of knowledge is a nice rhetorical trick, but it doesn't follow that all knowledge is of this form. For surely, some types of knowledge don't really contrast with true *belief* at all. Here are two examples that, at least at first sight, seem to be somewhat different in essence.

- **Know-how.** In Plato's distinction, the difference between knowledge and true belief is that the knowledge can be brought to account. But where know-how is concerned, the contrast is different; the difference between the man who, for example, knows how to drive a car and the man who merely believes he can is that the former can drive a car. If the latter can drive a car as well, then surely he knows how to drive a car; he may believe (and for some reason not know) *that* he can drive a car, but that is a different question. It is not clear, at first sight, that driving a car is a matter of *belief* at all.

- **Bodies of knowledge.** In common idiom, an encyclopaedia contains knowledge. If there is an agreed interpretation of the words in the book, the interpretation should entail that the words express things that are true and justifiable. But the encyclopaedia has no psychological states at all, and doesn't believe or disbelieve its contents. Beliefs or other psychological states need not come into it.

Why does Plato ignore these types of knowledge? The simple response is that he was chiefly concerned with establishing a distinction between true belief and knowledge, because his diagnosis of the ills of Athens had led him to worry that people were relying complacently on their beliefs about virtue and not seeking knowledge. Those whose beliefs about virtue happened to be true could teach virtue to the next generation; true beliefs don't lead one astray. However, how could it be known whose beliefs were true and whose false? Socrates showed that many of the most confident thinkers were mistaken. For Plato, it all came down to beliefs; other kinds of knowledge, if such there be, weren't the point.

There are more complex reasons, too. For example, with regard to know-how, Plato does discuss expertise in a number of places (e.g., *Theaetetus* 146ce), but he seems to have wanted a definition of knowledge as a single, unified phenomenon, of which different types of expertise would be species. This made it very difficult for him to do full justice to the heterogeneous nature of knowledge.

With regard to bodies of knowledge, Plato was very chary about written-down ideas. He believed that writing was a degenerate form of communication, and this no doubt influenced his adoption of the dialogue form. In the *Phaedrus*, Socrates says:

Writing shares a strange feature with painting. The offspring of painting stand there as if they were alive, but if anyone asks them anything, they are solemnly silent. The same is true of written words. You'd think they were speaking as if they had some understanding, but if you question anything that has been said because you want to learn more, it gives just the same message over and over. Once it has been written down, every discourse rolls about everywhere, reaching just as much those with understanding as those who have no business with it, and it does not know to whom it should speak and to whom not. And when it is faulted and attacked unfairly, it always needs its father's support; alone, it cannot defend itself or come to its own support.

(*Phaedrus*, 275d)

The written is infinitely less interesting to Plato than live discussion. But nowadays technology has blurred the distinction.

Some speech – as recorded on TV or radio – is as unchanging as a piece of text. One cannot interact with a recording; it will not change if one debates with it (it 'cannot come to its own support'). One can, of course, debate with the person who made the recording, but the recording will still stand. Like a piece of writing, a recorded utterance will remain in existence even if it has been exposed as a lie, or if its author has changed his mind. Like writing, it can be broadcast to a wide and undiscriminating audience (it 'rolls about everywhere'). None of these things seems particularly controversial to us, but to Plato they were the mark of a degenerate use of language that traded integrity for power. On the other hand, much written language today has speech-like features that Plato would have welcomed. E-mails and text messages allow a certain immediacy of interaction, while dynamically constructed Webpages present information to readers that is customised to their requirements and won't be circulated further.

Of course, there was no reason why Plato should be expected to anticipate such developments. As far as he was concerned, written communication is dead; its author may change his opinions, or the words may be misinterpreted with no way of putting the reader right. But it seems an odd view to hold in the present day, and therefore shouldn't count as a reason why a *modern* epistemologist should be opposed to treating bodies of knowledge as knowledge.[9]

Justified True Belief

I don't want to go into a detailed analysis of Plato's epistemological views (see Further Reading). The point I want to make is that already, in the first few years of the discipline of epistemology, its general features were in place. In the red corner, a sceptic who denies the possibility of knowledge; in the blue corner, JTB – an idea of knowledge as true belief supplemented by some sort of justification or holding to account. Very few well-known figures in epistemology since have attempted to break the hold of this vision of the debate over knowledge, even though the vision itself was the particular product of Plato's political reaction to a domestic reversal in a Greek city-state nearly two and a half millennia ago. I'll refer to this tradition in epistemology as the 'JTB tradition'.

I will include within the JTB tradition a number of philosophers who do not endorse as such the idea of knowledge as equivalent to justified true belief (as we have noted, this group includes Plato himself – see the *Theaetetus*, 201c–210d), but who follow Plato's general account that knowledge is true belief plus *something*, the 'something' turning 'mere' belief into knowledge. The JTB tradition is therefore firm that knowledge is a *psychological* state, which involves the person with knowledge assenting to or endorsing a *proposition*.

There is huge dispute amongst philosophers about what a proposition actually is, but for our purposes we can ignore this issue, because all are agreed that a proposition is expressed by a declarative sentence (i.e., one that says something about the world, not a question, command etc.). So propositional knowledge is knowledge *that* something or other is the case. And this does look very like a belief – an attitude towards a proposition.

For example, Sir A.J. Ayer devotes a whole chapter of his theory of knowledge to examining various different types, only to decide in the end – on the basis of what appears to be not very much – that knowledge is JTB after all.[10] Susan Haack moves straight into an impressive examination of the justification of beliefs (though in fairness it should be said that this is an interesting philosophical issue in its own right).[11]

Away from the mainstream, the American philosopher Fred Dretske tries to avoid the JTB definition, and instead analyses knowledge in terms of the information that caused the belief.[12] This is potentially a helpful move (as we shall see later on) but in this particular formulation doesn't get us very far. It is still the case that (a) something is known only when it is believed, (b) someone only knows something when they believe it, (c) what is known is true, and (d) it has a justification (in terms of information theory). In an important new work, Timothy Williamson breaks radically with the JTB *characterisation*, but stays within the JTB *tradition* by setting out from the assumption that knowing is a state of mind, and that knowing something in general entails believing it.[13] Even Wittgenstein continues to think primarily of beliefs, and sees his chief opponent as an epistemological sceptic.[14]

Nicholas Everitt and Alec Fisher (see Further Reading) produce a thorough survey of the efforts of philosophers to define the 'something extra',[15] but are forced to conclude that there is still, after two and a half millennia, no final consensus:

> [W]e have learned that there is universal agreement that knowledge requires truth. Secondly, there is an almost equally widespread agreement that knowledge requires belief. The disagreement arises on what more is required for knowledge than true belief.[16]

Surely another option open to us is to reject the analysis as a whole and step outside the JTB tradition. This is a radical step in the face of universal agreement. Why make it? Is there any reason for us to do it?

The Sceptic Bites Back

First of all, the animus of the JTB tradition has usually been focused on the sceptic. As we have seen, Plato was at least in part responding to sceptics, but scepticism can be much more thoroughgoing than that of Plato's opponents, Sophists such as Protagoras or quasi-Sophists like Gorgias. The earliest, really dedicated sceptic in intellectual history was Arcesilaus (*c*. 315–*c*. 240 BC), the first man who was positively in favour of withdrawing belief – and once you start questioning absolutely everything, it is not difficult to win arguments by destroying your opponent's position without advancing any positive thesis yourself.

At the basic level, everyone has wondered how they know they are not currently dreaming. René Descartes (1596–1650) famously tried to build philosophy on unassailable foundations by conducting a fictitious argument with a very bloody-minded sceptic who doubted everything; the attempt, sadly, foundered on the fact that most observers agree that the sceptic rather won the day. Indeed – I blush – even I once managed to prove, on the basis of some fairly innocuous premises, that everybody was dreaming all of the time![17]

It made sense for Plato to aim his arguments at sceptics, as they were prominent in Athenian political life at the time. It is less so for modern-day epistemologists, for no one occupies the sceptical position, except within academia. There are other purposes for epistemology, and other people who are interested in the arguments. Given the changing intellectual background, surely it would be better to reject scepticism as a type of philosophical disease (with Wittgenstein – see Note 14), and focus epistemological efforts on the areas where they can do some good and make a difference in the world.

Information Overload

When Plato was writing, scepticism was a serious political problem. Nowadays it is not. But his genius and lucidity have combined to cast a spell over the JTB tradition, and the same issues that preoccupied Plato are still being investigated, even though conditions have changed. Technological, economic and political developments that Plato could never have foreseen mean that epistemological theory needs to deal with different phenomena, and many epistemological assumptions could usefully be amended. 'The nature of knowledge cannot survive unchanged within this context of general transformation.'[18]

The new world to which epistemology needs to be applied is

characterised by a dramatic increase in the quantity of *data* that are being created and stored, as storage capacity has multiplied and cost diminished. When Plato was writing, the space required to store a work written on a scroll was large, the cost of reproducing it huge. Bound books reduced that space, and, once printing allowed the production of millions of volumes, libraries could hold them. Now, a floppy disk will hold a decent-sized book, a CD-ROM even more, and a laptop computer still more. More books are being written, and more periodicals published. More photographs are being taken, X-rays shot, videos made.

And the cost of storing all this material has shrunk rapidly. The new British Library in London, designed to hold 12 million volumes, cost £500 million. But magnetic storage is a different matter. A byte is the amount of storage required for a single character, so a book is 1 million bytes, or a megabyte. A gigabyte is the standard measure of data, a thousand megabytes (i.e., a thousand books). And the cost of storing a gigabyte of data magnetically was not much more than £5 in late 2000, and will be well under £1 by 2005, when the virtual equivalent of the British Library will cost a mere £12,000.

The opportunities this new technology has brought are already being exploited. To begin with, very little of the new material recorded in the world appears in print. As a consequence, the production of data has been 'democratised', in that most new stuff is created by individuals for a small audience: for example, office documents (80 per cent of all new paper documents), photographs (95 per cent of film documents) and camcorder tapes (20 per cent of magnetic tape storage). And it is the magnetically stored documents that are increasing in number; the use of paper and film for original content is remaining more or less constant.

Hence, whereas even 20 years ago the amount of data accessed (and created) by the ordinary citizen was relatively small, nowadays anyone living in a developed economy, with computers, electricity and reliable telephone or wireless connections, can get hold of colossal quantities of material, and can author a pretty huge amount as well. In all, as estimated by Hal Varian, humankind creates round about 1 exabyte of data annually. That is 1 *billion* gigabytes, or 1,000,000,000,000 books.

Which is not too far off 200 books' worth of data for every man, woman and child on the planet! Every *single* year![19]

This is not a world with which we, as yet, feel comfortable. We can all remember when people were starved of information; now we are drowning in it. If people had little or no access to the data they needed in the past, now we all know the feeling of having to trawl through pages and pages, documents and documents, to find just the exact thing we need. Having more data has not solved all our information requirements. It has merely given us *information overload*.

Will it be possible to deal more efficiently and intelligently with all these data? There are grounds for saying that it will. To see why, let's take a look at one of the influential technologies of the information revolution, the Internet.

The Internet and the World Wide Web

We all know the outer forms of the Internet: e-mails, the Web, newsgroups etc. We know we can contact our friends, do our banking through it, buy books or CDs. Some people say it will change our lives; others that it will make no difference at all. It is extraordinary, though, how few commentators are actually aware of the technology, and how prosaic it is.

The Internet is simply a network of computer networks, connected using the *Internet Protocol* (IP). IP enables a computer to take a file, break it up into slices called *packets*, and then send the packets to a destination (another computer) down a phone line using *dynamic routing* (i.e., making up routes to the destination, via various intermediaries, while the packets are in transit). Dynamic routing was a Cold War idea – if the intermediate computers were knocked out by enemy action, another route could be created. In practice, dynamic routing is useful in peacetime as it can steer packets around more standard equipment failures. The *Transmission Control Protocol* (TCP) tracks the packets, and the combination of protocols – the Internet standard – is called TCP/IP.

The public face of the Internet, most responsible for the Internet's take-off, is that fraction of the net called the *World Wide Web* (WWW or *the Web*). This is, in effect, a vast collection of files in multiple media – text, pictures, sounds, video, and so on. The Web works by storing the files on many different computers, called *servers*. It 'pretends' that the files on it are stored at a single source, by having a consistent system of addresses for the files, called *Uniform Resource Locators* (URL), which is what you type in the address box of your browser (the software that gives you a view of the Web, such as Internet Explorer, or Netscape Navigator). For example, the URL of Icon Books' Website is http://www.iconbooks.co.uk. Your computer gets at the file held at that URL by using (usually) the *Hypertext Transfer Protocol*, which is what the 'http' stands for. The use of HTTP makes it possible to access files stored anywhere in the world as if they were all held on a single giant host computer.

What makes the Web possible is its universal language, the *Hypertext Markup Language* (HTML), which structures a file so that your computer can lay out its data in the browser window, while also allowing it to contain links to other files – these are the *hyperlinks* generally highlighted in blue in a piece of text. Clicking on such links allows your computer to get at another file at another URL. Well-designed hyperlinks let you navigate through the Web looking at only the particular files you are interested in, unlike a standard text or video, where the structure is linear and you cannot easily hop about as you wish. HTML is an international standard, not owned by a particular company, and administered by the World Wide Web Consortium

(W3C), which helps the Web to be open both to readers *and* writers.

The openness of HTML allows pretty well anyone to create content and post it on the Web. The result has been an explosion of data. There are about 2.5 billion fixed documents on the Web, and when you add in all the databases that users can access through forms to create customised Webpages (e.g., the files that allow you to log on to your bank and see your own bank statements), that figure rises to 550 billion documents.

This is a huge amount of material (7.5 million gigabytes of data = 7,500,000,000 books). And this is just the Web; the Internet is far more than that! Needless to say, it is an unprecedented amount of information for people to have access to instantaneously. And it is this that has made the Internet the engine for a colossal shift in human capabilities.

Some commentators have refused to see the Internet as a significant enough change in technology to make it philosophically interesting; others have worried that the Internet will only bring problems. It is certainly important not to overstate the case for the defence, particularly in a world where half the population has never made a telephone call.[20] However, the sudden explosion of available content could be as significant to human development as the invention of movable type. As we have seen in this section, the actual technological developments aren't earth-shattering; a few transfer protocols here, a markup language there, and a system for managing changes and addresses. But, as with printing, a number of small changes, taken cumulatively, could have major effects.[21]

Knowledge, Technology and Organisations

Many of the Internet's small changes will be central to the knowledge economy. They will enable organisations to disperse knowledge across their members (employees, representatives, etc). This is essential – if knowledge is the key to competitive advantage, as we saw at the beginning of this book, then it has to be used well and efficiently by organisations.

Can an organisation *possess* knowledge? Does it make sense to say that? Recall that the JTB tradition in epistemology says that knowing is a *psychological* state, that it is something done only by people.

Well, there is certainly one uncontroversial way in which an organisation can be said to possess knowledge (possibly metaphorically), and that is if it employs someone who unambiguously has that knowledge. Let us imagine a fictitious firm, Worldwide Manufacturing; suppose it makes a particular type of widget, type X, and it employs Smith, an expert in X, in its London office. Then we can say that Worldwide Manufacturing contains or possesses knowledge about X, in this case in the person of Smith. If Smith goes, Worldwide Manufacturing would no longer contain that knowledge. This is pretty straightforward at this stage – nothing about the situation contradicts the JTB theory.

Now consider a second stage. WM executives realise that Smith is a scarce resource – he goes on holiday, he sleeps at night, he has coffee breaks, all of which mean that his expertise is not always available. Furthermore, he is based in London, whereas WM is a multinational; if something goes wrong with its X-factory in São Paolo, it will at best be difficult to employ Smith's expertise, with time differences, logistical problems of getting the knowledge from London to São Paolo in time, and a language problem – Smith speaks no Portuguese.

As a result, WM undertakes a *knowledge acquisition* exercise. This involves specialists interviewing Smith and creating a system that apes his expertise in X. This could be a computer system, but we will suppose it is a set of interlinked Webpages designed to mimic Smith's problem-solving behaviour. If something goes wrong on the X-assembly line, the manager can look up the appropriate page, which will tell him or her what to do. When there are different possibilities, there will be a choice of links to take the user to the appropriate page. The way the user *navigates* through the set of Webpages will track the way that Smith diagnoses problems in X and sorts them out. These Webpages can then be posted on WM's corporate *Intranet* (i.e., a private section of the Internet, accessible only with a password), and so – via an automatic translation system – are immediately accessible to the non-experts in São Paolo and elsewhere who need to know about X. They will also be accessible to people in London who might need Smith's expertise after office hours or during his holidays.

After this second stage, we can still say that WM contains Smith's knowledge. Smith works for WM, as at the first stage. It is just that WM is more efficient about sending Smith's knowledge around the firm.

But now consider a third stage, when Smith retires, or is poached by WM's rivals. WM does not have to stop making X-type widgets; neither does it have to employ a new expert. Smith's expertise is still available to engineers 24 hours a day, seven days a week, as long as they have a laptop and a phone line. The Intranet is still running the Webpages about X-type widgets, and their navigation structure causes the user to go through the same problem-solving process that Smith would have gone through.

Now, earlier on, we used the phrase, 'WM contains knowledge about X', loosely, metaphorically, knowing there was an easy rationalisation of it, since Smith was an employee of WM. Now, however, we cannot be so loose, because Smith has left. No person within the organisation has Smith's problem-solving capability. The people who drew up the Webpages were most likely independent consultants who have long since gone; let us further suppose that nothing has ever gone wrong with an X-type widget, and that therefore no one in WM has ever even read the Webpages. No one in WM has any justified true beliefs about problems with X-type widgets.

And yet, it is very intuitive to say that WM still contains, or possesses the knowledge about, X. If there is any difficulty with an X-type widget in Brazil or England or Russia or India or Nigeria, the WM engineer on the spot will be able to find out from WM's corporate Intranet exactly what to do. The knowledge available for the engineer is so much more than he or she would get from a book about X, in that the engineer, together with the links that organise the Intranet, will solve the problem. The engineer need not read all the Webpages; instead it is the *organisation of the Website* that provides the expertise that previously Smith used to provide.

It looks like we would have to say that any epistemology that is to be *applicable* in this context should allow for *organisations* as well as people possessing knowledge in a non-metaphorical way. It would certainly be possible for an alternative analysis to be developed, or the JTB tradition defended (see the final section); but epistemology will be that much more valuable in the knowledge economy if epistemologists take its concerns seriously, and don't try to analyse them away. As Lyotard puts it:

We may thus expect a thorough exteriorization of knowledge with respect to the 'knower,' at whatever point he or she may occupy in the knowledge process. The old principle that the acquisition of knowledge is indissociable from the training of minds, or even of individuals, is becoming obsolete ... The relationship of the suppliers and users of knowledge to the knowledge they supply and use is now tending ... to assume the form already taken by the relationship of commodity producers and consumers to the commodities they produce and consume – that is, the form of value.[22]

And indeed, we shouldn't end this section without noting that in the social sciences, treating an organisation as an agent in its own right, greater than the sum of the people who make up that organisation, with its own goals, methods and values, would not be unusual. The JTB tradition would need an update to retain consistency with such thinking.[23]

Managing Knowledge

The knowledge possessed by an organisation is an *asset* of that organisation. I mean by this that the knowledge is a claim on future benefits. The organisation *invests* money in the acquisition of a knowledge asset (e.g., by beginning a programme of research and development) in the hope that this investment will pay dividends by increasing future effectiveness (or profits, in the case of a firm).

Like any asset, the knowledge an organisation possesses needs to be managed properly in order to realise the anticipated benefits. This is where the insights of epistemology will be of enormous value, as an understanding of the properties and dynamics of knowledge is essential to knowing how best to use knowledge for an organisation's general benefit.

An example: on 23 August 2001, the famous pottery company Royal Doulton announced a half-yearly loss of £9 million and placed its factories on a four-day week; its shares had fallen to a fifth of their 1998 value. One major factor in its decline was that it had failed to spot trends in the ceramics market. For instance, over the last few years, British diners have abandoned the big family dinner in favour of TV dinners, meals out, meals *al fresco*, and generally more casual dining. However, Doulton had continued to produce sets of matching china, rather than individual pieces available at supermarkets and other convenient outlets. It did not know what its customers wanted; its half-yearly report admitted to 'weaknesses in its information systems'.

What is going on? Doulton employs about 3,000 people in Stoke-on-Trent, almost all of whom will have been well aware of – indeed part of – the trend away from set-piece meals. Poor *management* of that knowledge, possessed by nearly all of its employees, meant that the changes in dining patterns were never taken account of by management. As a result, the company made losses, and people's jobs are at risk.[24]

What sorts of issue are involved in managing knowledge? A

recent UK scientific research project, Advanced Knowledge Technologies (AKT), has characterised knowledge management as six challenges. These are as follows – and to show that they are not merely management issues, I have annotated them with meaty and classic epistemological questions, given in italics.

- **Acquisition.** The initial problem with knowledge is when and how to acquire it. We can distinguish three levels of acquisition. First, there is knowledge that currently does not exist and would have to be discovered by a programme of research (e.g., a cure for AIDS). Second, there is knowledge that exists, but is not possessed by the organisation. Third, there is knowledge that is possessed by the organisation, but in the wrong form (e.g., in our example from the previous section, Smith's knowledge of X-type widgets was held inconveniently in his head, and a decision to acquire the knowledge from him and place it in a set of Webpages was taken). The management decisions here depend on the difficulty of acquiring the knowledge (does a suitable code exist?), the costs of the acquisition, and the projected benefits. *How can we know what we don't know? How can we know what we need to know? How can different types of knowledge be justified?*

- **Modelling.** Once acquired, knowledge has to be stored in a useful way. The representation must be such that it is easy to write the knowledge down as it comes in, and equally easy to read the knowledge once it is acquired. *How should different types of knowledge best be represented? How far does changing a representation change the knowledge?*

- **Retrieval.** When an organisation has a large repository of knowledge, it must be possible to get at the knowledge quickly enough for it to be of use. This means that the repository must be structured to allow a quick, reliable and efficient search of its contents. If the knowledge disappears in a pile of other stuff – like the Ark of the Covenant in the final scene of *Raiders of the Lost Ark* – it is as good as forgotten. *How best to organise connected pieces of knowledge? How do they relate to each other?*

- **Re-use.** If some knowledge is present in a firm, people who need that knowledge need to know how to get hold of it, so they don't go about re-acquiring knowledge expensively (or incompetently, like Royal Doulton). *How do we recognise knowledge that we need and don't have? How do pieces of knowledge relate to each other?*

- **Publishing.** It is essential that the people who need knowledge get it at the right time. Too soon, and it contributes to their information overload; too late, and ... well, it's too late. They also need it in the right form. Someone who needs one little piece of technical information does not need either a whole set of explanations for beginners or a highly rarefied piece of theory. *Does changing the way knowledge is visualised change the knowledge? How do we know what we need to know?*

- **Maintenance.** Having developed a repository of knowledge, it has to be kept running and up to date. This involves a series of disparate issues, such as: verifying that the knowledge is correct, and that the representation correctly represents the knowledge; updating the knowledge to keep track of changes in the domain; 'forgetting' knowledge that is misleading or out of date; altering formats as the organisation's needs change; maybe even packaging and selling the knowledge if it would be valuable for outsiders. *How do we know that an account of the world is correct? How do we know that a sentence correctly represents a proposition? What is the logical relation between statements, and how can the effects of the removal of a statement be tracked? How can different types of knowledge be justified?*[25]

These challenges all involve epistemological problems, many of which have long been the object of study in traditional epistemology, others of which are new, still others old problems with newly acquired significance. But this is a context where the application of epistemology would be extremely timely. The problems of scepticism, which have driven so much epistemological research, are very much less pressing.

Data, Information and Knowledge

Is this to say that everything that appears on the Internet, or in corporate disk space, is to be called knowledge? Is every item in a symbolic code knowledge – even those items that are unreadable or useless?

Of course, that is not the idea. What we want to sort out is which items are worthy of epistemological investigation. We will focus on computer-based items, although the same distinctions that we are about to draw will apply to paper-based materials, and even to thoughts and beliefs.

Let us begin by examining the basic content in a computer – a set of symbols; we can call this **data**. Data can be any old garbage, and so may be useful or may not. A subclass of data we can call **information**, which is those data that have an *interpretation*, or which make *sense*. Of course, the attribution of meaning to something is a deep and complex philosophical problem in itself, but let's assume that we can draw some sort of a distinction between meaningless stuff and meaningful stuff. In the case of Webpages, meaningful stuff can of course include pictures and video, as well as text.

How might information contrast with knowledge? Let's try to suggest a distinction by the use of an example.

For several years now, supermarkets have recorded the details of each purchase made in them by using electronic tills, each of which updates a central database. As a result, supermarkets with nationwide chains of branches have enormous masses of data about billions and billions of purchases. These data are clearly information, as the big databanks will have some interpretation which enables the reader to work out which purchase is referred to, what was purchased, how much it cost, etc.

Is this vast quantity of information useful in itself? Hardly. No human reader could scan the printouts in a lifetime, even if he wanted to, still less draw any conclusions from it. If such stuff is knowledge, then there doesn't seem to be much point in having it.

However, one can imagine converting such data-sets into knowledge (this would be a knowledge acquisition process, in the terms of the previous section). Using special computer programs called *machine learning programs*, or *induction programs*, a computer can trawl through enormous data-sets and extract statistical relationships between some of the data. These relationships can then be published as sets of rules, which might look something like this:

- People in Hertfordshire spend more per visit to the supermarket than people in Berkshire.

- People in Inner London who buy beer are more likely to buy crisps simultaneously.

- People in the South-West have become keener on branded tinned food over the last five years.

What I would like to suggest now is that these probabilistic inductions are not only information but **knowledge**. They are knowledge because they are *usable*, because they can be translated into *effective action*. They are not, let's face it, terribly exciting, but they will help a supermarket save money on deliveries, warehousing and marketing by sending goods where they are most likely to be sold quickly. It is not an exact science, by any means, but there is some payoff for this sort of activity, and it would not be possible without the collection of the giant data-sets through the electronic tills.

Note further that none of this need ever appear as anyone's *belief*. The content of the data-sets is obviously collected independently of any human operator. The machine learning program will extract the knowledge without consulting anyone. And the knowledge thus extracted might easily be translated into managerial actions (e.g., changes in orders of wholesale goods) automatically, without any human managerial interference.

And it is knowledge of this sort that organisations such as supermarkets have to manage. There is an investment in the collection of those data and in running the hardware and software that makes it possible, and organisations need to know whether the investment is worth it. The reader can satisfy himself or herself that the six challenges of knowledge management will apply here. Dealing effectively with bodies of knowledge of this sort will make a big difference to the profits of commercial firms and to the success of non-commercial organisations.

So, let's recap our characterisation. Data are sets of symbols, while information is meaningful data. Knowledge is that information which is usable for the purposes of supporting or suggesting action; it is a stepping stone to some end.

Data, information, knowledge: they sit as a pyramid. Perhaps, with tongue only slightly in cheek, one might even imagine wisdom sitting at the apex, characterised as the ability to select appropriate important goals for one's useful knowledge to be applied to.

Scepticism is out of place here. The supermarket of our example wants help with the six challenges of knowledge management. A proof that, say, the external world exists and that the five senses can deliver knowledge, reassuring and philosophically interesting though this may be, is not going to be of any help in deciding how many tins of beans to send to Wiltshire. The manager who doubted the existence of Wiltshire would be given a long rest, not a proof.

The Semantic Web

This characterisation of knowledge – as usable information – has been generally adopted by those researching knowledge management in the Internet age. By creating technologies that help in the handling of information, more information becomes usable, and therefore by our criteria, turns from information to knowledge. Hence technologists, such as W3C, or the AKT project mentioned earlier, who have taken the 'usable information' characterisation on board, can produce real systems and tools that actively help organisations and individuals become more effective by controlling the information they have access to. Information overload is alleviated, not by reducing the amount of information available, but by increasing the amount of knowledge.

W3C has developed a language for writing Webpages to supersede HTML, a language called XML (eXtensible Markup Language – actually a language for representing other languages, but let's steer clear of details!). XML allows designers to place 'tags' in Webpages that are invisible to the reader (i.e., they don't appear in the browser when the Webpage is being read), but which *can* be read by a computer. These tags can then 'tell' the user's computer what the number or the word is about. Contrast this with HTML, which simply tells the computer where to place the data on-screen.

A browser that is XML-enabled (i.e., can cope with XML) will be able to search not just for key words on the page but also taking into account their underlying meaning, as represented by the tags. So, whereas currently a search engine will come up with, say, 10,000 hits, with XML it might come up with only 20 hits, but they will be the 20 you want, because they will be tagged with the subject area of your interest. If your interest is in Kate Bush, then typing in 'Bush' together with some specification of your musical requirements, the engine will ignore all the George Bushes, Shepherd's Bushes, rose bushes, African bushes, etc. The new search will be much more sensitive to the *context* of the query.

That in itself would give the user of the Internet much more control of the information received. As it stands, XML is a comparative infant, but telling computers what Webpages are about is an idea that will surely be exploited in a large number of currently undreamt-of ways. The interpretation of Web-based text and images, currently a human responsibility, could at least partly be done automatically. This will allow projects like AKT to write software that can provide information (e.g., flight information) and world-altering services (e.g., ticket-buying agents), ushering in *context-sensitive knowledge services* – ways of providing people and organisations with the technology to solve their particular knowledge problems as they happen, and as they need solutions.

Most of these services would ordinarily be done by a person – the difference is not that new work gets done, but that it gets done quickly, automatically, in a standard way, and exhaustively (i.e., an agent can search the entire Web for the best price for an air ticket, in a fraction of a second). Information overload would be alleviated by the reduction of routine tasks, and the standardisation of non-routine tasks.

This conception of the World Wide Web augmented by XML is called the *Semantic Web,* and is based entirely on the new characterisation of knowledge. Without the recognition of the epistemological importance of usable information, such a conception might never have arisen. It certainly has nothing to do with JTB. Many of these developments will seem small-scale and technical, but they are powerful and cumulatively important, and they would not have come about without the change in approach to the problem of knowledge.

Knowledge: Justified?

So, we have established a rival conception of knowledge, and furthermore one that has been the driver of important developments in technology. What is the relationship between the 'usable information' conception of knowledge and the JTB tradition?

One thing that has often been remarked upon in the history of epistemology is that the nature of the justification of a belief sufficient to convert it to knowledge (or the 'something extra' required in the stead of justification) is highly problematic. Even leaving aside some fiendish thought experiments developed by Edmund Gettier in the 1960s that cast doubt on any reasonable notion of justification as being sufficient – experiments which no one has satisfactorily explained away – there has never been any consensus about what justification would do.[26]

Even under the 'usable information' characterisation, some sort of justification of the knowledge's efficacy would be required. The quality of a stock-control system will affect a firm's profits and its employees' jobs; the quality of a heart-monitoring system will affect a person's chances of life. In such sensitive contexts, the knowledge that has been put into the computer had better be reliable.

But there is a difference in the role of the justification under the two characterisations. In the JTB tradition, the justification is central – a true belief is knowledge if and only if the justification of the belief is adequate. Philosophers have suggested a number of possible types of justification. Examples include: the knowledge can be derived from some privileged, deep foundational knowledge from which all knowledge must spring; the knowledge was discovered using reliable techniques; the knowledge is part of a coherent picture of the world. There is no consensus about which, if any, is correct.

Under the 'usable information' view, on the other hand, a justification is a kind of certificate that the knowledge could be the basis for action of some type. It would be the proof that the information being discussed was usable. However, the existence of the proof would be required, not to turn the information into knowledge, but to demonstrate that the information was usable and reliable. Often, of course, usability requires a demonstration of reliability – as with computers in sensitive contexts. But the existence of a justification, or proof, or anything extra over and above the usefulness of the information, is not *conceptually* bound up with the identification of information with knowledge.

Interestingly, Plato discusses the possibility of such a pragmatic definition of knowledge in the *Theaetetus* 167ab. The idea that epistemologists might be concerned with which knowledge is worth knowing – as opposed to which knowledge is legitimised by various different technical accounts of knowledge – has not been pursued much since, but Plato does give the issue profound thought in the *Theaetetus* 172b–177c. (He would no doubt disagree with our conclusions here, though.)

Knowledge: True?

Usable information that is propositional will (usually if not all the time) be true. In our supermarket example, if the propositions induced by the machine-learning program (e.g., that people in Hertfordshire spend more, etc.) actually turn out to be false, the supermarket will make poor decisions based on this misinformation. Its acting on these false propositions will be likely, all else being equal, to reduce its profits. Hence, the information will not be usable in the way required by our characterisation; it will not be able to underlie *effective* action.

Does this mean that all knowledge is true according to our characterisation? Recall that this is universally agreed in traditional epistemology (Everitt and Fisher, pp. 48–9). Does the new epistemology that we are proposing here fall in with the consensus?

The answer, interestingly, is 'no': one can act effectively on information that is not strictly true.

To take an initial and obvious example: much of the knowledge that is required in industry is know-how rather than propositional knowledge. It is knowledge that can help achieve something. Hence it is of an imperative form (first do *this*, then *this*, then *this*, if you want to achieve *that*), rather than the propositional form (*this* is the case), which is more usually associated with truth and falsity. The imperative form can be useful or not useful, appropriate or inappropriate, but not strictly true or false.

A second example of knowledge that is not true is what is called *default* reasoning. We rely on default reasoning to an enormous degree in our problem-solving. The idea of default reasoning is that you can treat generalisations as universally true, even when they are not. So, for example, when told that Tweety is a bird, we deduce that Tweety flies, based on our knowledge that all birds fly. The reasoning is sound. Only one problem: it is not true that all birds fly (penguins and ostriches don't, for a start), and if we later find out that Tweety happens to be a penguin, then we will withdraw the conclusion that he flies. This is default reasoning.

In general, default reasoning has been ignored by philosophers (with honourable exceptions). It was first properly examined by computer scientists trying to develop machines with artificial intelligence, who were faced by the practical realisation that default reasoning is used all the time.[27] We blithely assume that all elephants are grey, all rooms have floors, all cars have four wheels, all tigers have four legs, all chairs can be sat on, all restaurants charge customers for food, etc. These propositions are all false (it is not true that *all* rooms have floors, because when my house was being renovated, the kitchen had no floor; and so on with the other examples). But surely, if we know anything, it is that rooms have floors. The information provided by these propositions – the essential inferences they allow us to make – justifies this conclusion.

A third example is that of *heuristic* reasoning. This is reasoning by rule of thumb, and is a vital part of the knowledge of experts in particular fields (i.e., of *expertise*). Much expertise consists of getting the right answer quickly with the minimum of investigation. For example, given a medical dictionary and a functioning laboratory most of us could diagnose an illness eventually. The problem would be that it would take so long, the patient would probably be dead by the time we knew what he had. The expert diagnostician, on the other hand, has to pinpoint the disease quickly enough to treat it. In order to achieve that speed, the diagnostician will bundle together a lump of medical knowledge into a quick-and-dirty rule, which will tell him that, for example, if a patient has a white-blood-cell count of x, and a certain set of antibodies present, he probably has a disease from a particular class. This is a *heuristic*, and is literally false, in that the patient could have that particular white-blood-cell count and that particular antibody and yet not have the disease. Clearly, heuristic reasoning is related to default reasoning; the distinction is that the heuristics are less likely to be borne out by events. They are not deep-down assumptions but clever shortcuts developed professionally as part of the execution of expertise.

Each of these types of information, I am claiming, should be seen as knowledge, in that they are all extremely usable for effective action. Everyone uses know-how and default reasoning; experts rely on heuristics. Can an epistemologist possibly ignore these?

Knowledge: Belief?

Perhaps the most radical departure I am proposing is that knowledge need not be a psychological state. There are philosophers who are prepared to take a smaller step, that knowledge isn't a belief – for example, Timothy Williamson (see Note 13). The requirements of the Internet age, however, are stronger than that. Knowledge does not have to be anything psychological at all.

As we have seen from the widget example earlier, from the point of view of an organisation and its need to manage its knowledge effectively to get the maximum benefit from it, there is no essential difference between the organisation possessing

knowledge via its employees, and its possessing it via some artificial means (e.g., an Intranet, manuals, organisational procedures, etc.).

Seen from the JTB tradition, the widget example changes
radically as we go through the various stages. When there is an
expert on X-type widgets in the firm, there is a (merely)
metaphorical sense in which the firm can be said to possess the
knowledge; when the expert leaves, then there is no person
within the firm with any knowledge; the two situations are completely different. *This surely renders the JTB tradition useless
from the point of view of those who need to understand and
manage their knowledge in an organisational context.*
Epistemologically, the organisation is interested only in its capabilities, not in how those capabilities are manifested. In other
words, it is the 'belief' element of JTB, rather than the 'justified'
or 'true' bit, that has most to do with rendering the JTB tradition ineffective as a tool for understanding the requirements of
the knowledge economy which we set out at the beginning of
this book.

Conclusion: Twenty-first Century Alchemy?

To review our analysis, we have examined the JTB tradition in
the context of the knowledge economy, and found it wanting.
An epistemology suitable for this technological climate can be
fairly relaxed about justification; knowledge should be justified,
but different types of knowledge will need different types of justification. The requirement for truth needs to be replaced with a
requirement for effectiveness (which will, one imagines, coincide
with truth to a large extent). The analysis of knowledge as a
belief, or as any psychological state, seriously undermines the
JTB tradition in the modern context.

The proposal is that the JTB characterisation be replaced by
the characterisation of knowledge as 'usable information'. We
have illustrated the ideas here, although of course what has

transpired in this essay falls a long way short of a tight definition. No doubt, giving such a definition to the new conception of knowledge will be as difficult as the task of refining the JTB conception has been. However, technologists such as W3C and AKT have been able to use 'usable information' as a practical guide to understanding the problems of knowledge management, and developing technologies that can help alleviate those problems.

There are responses that a philosopher of the JTB tradition can make. A *heroic response* asserts that the traditional analysis of knowledge defines what knowledge is, and therefore usable information cannot be knowledge (however interesting or important it may be). This, in effect, says that whatever problems there are in the knowledge economy, *we're* not going to help you with them.

There is no argument against this response, of course; it is perfectly self-consistent. But we have seen from the account of the knowledge management challenges that there are serious and interesting epistemological problems associated with them, and it would be disappointing were our cry for help refused.

More constructive is an *analytic response* which would review our examples and try to show that they 'really' are examples of JTB in some way or other. For example, this response would attempt to show that some of our 'false' knowledge is really true when you understand it properly, or that what seem to be non-beliefs are actually reducible to psychological states in some way.

Though it takes our concerns more seriously, this isn't a great improvement on the heroic response. Its underlying premise, that epistemology is more or less okay once we realise that we have misconstrued the significance of our 'counter-examples', fails to take into account the essential need for experts to reach out to their constituency, rather than the other way round. An expert, whether an epistemologist, physicist, astrologer or car mechanic, must tailor his or her expertise to the people who need it, not vice versa. It is not for the busy corporate executive or NGO director to try to fit their knowledge problems into the JTB framework; rather, it is the job of the epistemologist to show how the JTB theory applies to the problems as they appear on the ground. Any devious analysis is, in a sense, the 'hidden wiring' that the user of the theory must not be bothered with.

But, if we are to face up to the facts, the Internet and related technological innovations have changed the way knowledge is viewed. In Plato's day, when the JTB tradition began, knowledge was a personal accomplishment, and so it continued pretty well up to the present. But there has been a gradual change, so that knowledge is now also a commodity, to be bought, sold, managed, invested in, leveraged, deployed, etc. We need an epistemology appropriate for this context, and the JTB tradition isn't it.

Of course, I have been describing a world of new technology and buzzwords that may be a passing fad. It may be thought that if JTB sits tight and ignores present circumstances, it will regain its applicability. This is certainly possible, but doesn't detract from the need for an information-based epistemology now, and the mere fact that the knowledge economy may disappear next week shows neither that it has no pressing epistemological requirements, nor that any epistemological discoveries made in that context will have no wider interest or application.

In short, there is a need for an epistemology tailored for a specific audience which the JTB tradition has failed to deliver, and it is in danger of missing a real opportunity to move from academe into a constructive engagement with the world of commerce and technology.

It may be that epistemology now is in the position of the philosophy of matter in the late medieval period. Philosophers had always had theories of what the world was made of, from the times of the ancient Greeks to the alchemists, and these theories came under the heading of 'natural philosophy'. However, in the seventeenth century, particularly thanks to

Newton, natural philosophy gradually acquired an empirical basis, and found itself debating, not antiquated thought experiments about how far you could divide space or substance, but problems such as the correct description of the orbits of the planets. It is certainly not the case that the alchemists made no contribution to our understanding of matter, but it cannot be denied that if you want to find out about what makes up our world, you would be wiser to ask a physicist or a chemist. Natural philosophy gradually transmuted into hard science.

There are resemblances between epistemology now and natural philosophy then. After millennia of relatively inconclusive debate, there is for the first time a basis and a requirement for empirical application of ideas. Some of these ideas will be of great use in this new world, others will turn out to be useless. My guess, and I can't say I know this, is that the JTB tradition will turn out to be a dead end – the alchemy of our day.

Notes

1. There are many works defending this switch to the 'new' economy. For instance, Thomas A. Stewart, *Intellectual Capital: The New Wealth of Organizations* (London: Nicholas Brealey Publishing, 1997), Leif Edvinsson and Michael S. Malone, *Intellectual Capital* (London: Piatkus, 1997), Thomas H. Davenport and Laurence Prusak, *Working Knowledge: How Organizations Manage What They Know* (Boston: Harvard Business School Press, 1997). A more philosophical analysis is Jean-François Lyotard, *The Postmodern Condition: A Report on Knowledge* (Manchester: Manchester University Press, 1984).

2. See Joseph Stiglitz, 'Scan Globally, Reinvent Locally: Knowledge Infrastructure and the Localisation of Knowledge', in Diane Stone (ed.), *Banking on Knowledge: The Genesis of the Global Development Network* (London: Routledge, 2000), pp. 24–43, and other papers in that volume.

3. Alan Burton-Jones, *Knowledge Capitalism: Business, Work and Learning in the New Economy* (Oxford: Oxford University Press, 1999), pp. 8–9.

4. I am using the term 'sceptic' loosely here to describe anyone who, for whatever reason, doubted the veracity of objective knowledge. 'Sceptic' can also denote, in a more narrow sense, particular schools of philosophy such as the Pyrrhonists and the Academic sceptics (of whom Cicero was one).

5. I am not, in this book, going to supply the biographical context of Plato's work, interesting though that is. A small and neat summary of Plato's life is given in R. M. Hare, *Plato* (Oxford: Oxford University Press, 1982, Past Masters series), pp. 1–8.

6. Socrates left no writings. His execution, on conviction for the corruption of youth (i.e. spreading dissension, rather than any more lurid crime), appalled Plato, and many of the early works are defences of and justifications for Socrates' philosophical method.

7. It is standard academic practice to refer to passages in Plato via the numbering of the early edition by Stephanus. These are given in the margin of most editions of Plato's works.

8. For a discussion of the interpretative difficulties, see Robin Waterfield's essay in his edition of the *Theaetetus* (Harmondsworth: Penguin, 1987), pp. 218–25, which includes the classic references.

9. For an interesting discussion of this ancient prejudice against writing see Jorge Luis Borges, 'On the Cult of Books', in *The Total Library: Non-Fiction 1922–1986*, ed. Eliot Weinberger, trans. Esther Allen and Suzanne Jill Levine (London: Penguin, 2000), pp. 358–62.

10. A. J. Ayer, *The Problem of Knowledge* (Harmondsworth: Penguin, 1956), pp. 7–35.

11. Susan Haack, *Evidence and Inquiry: Towards Reconstruction in Epistemology* (Oxford: Blackwell, 1993).

12. Fred I. Dretske, *Knowledge and the Flow of Information* (Oxford: Blackwell, 1981), pp. 85–106.

13. Timothy Williamson, *Knowledge and its Limits* (Oxford: Clarendon Press, 2000).

14. Ludwig Wittgenstein, *On Certainty* (Oxford: Blackwell, 1969), ed. Gertrude E. M. Anscombe, G. H. von Wright and Denis Paul.

15. Nicholas Everitt and Alec Fisher, *Modern Epistemology: A New Introduction* (New York: McGraw-Hill, 1995), pp. 17–50.

16. Ibid., pp. 48–9.

17. This is not, perhaps, a major moment in intellectual history, but for the record the paper in question is: Kieron O'Hara, 'Sceptical Overkill: On Two Recent Arguments Against Scepticism', *Mind*, vol. 102 (1993), pp. 315–27. For Descartes, see the *Meditations on First Philosophy*, particularly the first meditation, which is in a number of editions, including John Cottingham, Robert Stoothoff and Dugald Murdoch (eds), *The Philosophical Writings of Descartes: Volume II* (Cambridge: Cambridge University Press, 1985), pp. 1–62.

18. Lyotard, op. cit., p. 4.

19. Most of the figures in this section have been taken from Varian's heroic – and entertaining – study, available at http://www.sims.berkeley.edu/research/projects/how-much-info/summary.html.

20. Statistic from Matthew Symonds, 'Haves and Have Nots', in 'Government and the Internet' survey, *The Economist* (24 June 2000), pp. 19–23.

21. For a dismissive account of the Internet, see Gordon Graham, *The Internet: A Philosophical Inquiry* (London: Routledge, 1999). I have criticised this book in a review (written with Louise Crow) in *International Studies in the Philosophy of Science*, vol. 15 (2001), and in an article on 'Democracy and the Internet', in the Web journal *Ends and Means*, at http://www.abdn.ac.uk/philosophy/cpts/ohara.hti. For a

worry about the effects on democracy and free speech, see Cass Sunstein, *Republic.com* (Princeton: Princeton University Press, 2001). The classic account of the effect of printing on Western civilisation is Marshall McLuhan, *The Gutenberg Galaxy* (Toronto: University of Toronto Press, 1962).

22. Lyotard, op. cit., p. 4.

23. Examples of important and interesting works on organisations include Kenneth J. Arrow, *The Limits of Organization* (New York: Norton, 1974) and Mary Douglas, *How Institutions Think* (London: Routledge, 1987). Charles Jonscher writes very well about the importance of retaining the human element in such discussions in *Wiredlife: Who Are We in the Digital Age?* (London: Anchor, 1999).

24. 'The China Syndrome', *The Economist* (25 August 2001), p. 33.

25. Longer discussions of these six challenges can be found at the AKT Website at http://www.aktors.org.

26. The Gettier experiments appear in Edmund Gettier, 'Is Justified True Belief Knowledge?', *Analysis*, vol. 23 (1963), pp. 121–3. This paper is reprinted in a couple of more accessible collections of philosophical essays, and Everitt and Fisher discuss the arguments in *Modern Epistemology*, op. cit., pp. 21–9.

27. Raymond Reiter, 'A Logic for Default Reasoning', *Artificial Intelligence*, vol. 13 (1980), pp. 81–132.

Further Reading

A good general survey of and introduction to epistemology is Nicholas Everitt and Alec Fisher, *Modern Epistemology: A New Introduction* (New York: McGraw-Hill, 1995).

In this book I have touched upon only a few of the issues raised by Plato's philosophy. Dave Robinson and Judy Groves, *Introducing Plato* (Cambridge: Icon Books, 2000), gives a general overview of his work and influence. One of the many virtues of Plato is that he is one of the few philosophers who can be read for pleasure. To read Plato's epistemological works, start with W.K.C. Guthrie (trans.), *Protagoras and Meno* (London: Penguin, 1956). Both are useful, but the *Meno* is particularly important. More difficult, but central to understanding Plato's epistemology, is the *Theaetetus*: see Robin Waterfield (trans.), *Theaetetus* (London: Penguin, 1987), or Myles Burnyeat (ed.), *The Theaetetus of Plato* (Indianapolis: Hackett, 1990), which contains the text translated by M.J. Levett. The important book-length essays by Waterfield and Burnyeat are invaluable for the student of Plato, and give a good guide to the issues and the literature. Another useful early piece is Walter Hamilton (trans.), *Gorgias* (London: Penguin, 1960).

The history and general pattern of scepticism is given in the essays in Myles Burnyeat (ed.), *The Skeptical Tradition* (Berkeley: University of California Press, 1983).

A nice little reference book for the Internet is John Cowpertwait and Simon Flynn, *The Internet from A to Z* (Cambridge: Icon Books, 2001). I particularly like the appendix on emoticons or smileys. An altogether heftier tome is Margaret Levine Young, Doug Muder, Dave Kay, Kathy Warfel and Alison Burrows, *Internet: Millenium Edition: The Complete Reference* (Berkeley: Osborne McGraw-Hill, 1999, but regularly updated).

Charles Jonscher, *Wiredlife: Who Are We in the Digital Age?* (London: Anchor, 1999), is an excellent history of information technology, with an important focus on the human element.

The knowledge economy, and the way it rewards creativity, is discussed in John Howkins, *The Creative Economy: How People Make Money From Ideas* (London: Penguin, 2001).

A perceptive analysis, or prediction, of the effect of technology on knowledge is in the classic Jean-François Lyotard, *The Postmodern Condition: A Report on Knowledge*, translated by Geoffrey Bennington and Brian Massumi, with a foreword by Fredric Jameson (Manchester: Manchester University Press, 1984).

The World Wide Web Consortium (W3C) administers HTML; its website is at http://www.w3c.org. A brief, clear statement of the importance of XML can be found in Tim Berners-Lee, James Hendler and Ora Lassila, 'The Semantic Web', *Scientific American*, May 2001, available at http://www.scientificamerican.com/2001/0501issue/0501berners-lee.html. The manifesto of the AKT project is available at http://www.aktors.org/publications/Manifesto.doc.

Perhaps the most influential book on knowledge management of late is Ikujiro Nonaka and Hirotaka Takeuchi, *The Knowledge-Creating Company: How Japanese Companies Create the Dynamics of Innovation* (Oxford: Oxford University Press, 1995).

Key Ideas

Data are collections of symbols.

Epistemology is the philosophical study of knowledge. It addresses questions such as: what knowledge is; what kinds of knowledge there are; where knowledge comes from; whether there are things that we can't know; how we can know what we don't know, and look for it. Clearly such issues are strongly related, for example, to the study of science and how science progresses. A great deal of epistemological research has been aimed at confounding *scepticism*. Plato was the first epistemologist of any note; a list of greats would include Aristotle, Descartes, Spinoza, Leibniz, Locke, Berkeley, Hume, Kant, J.S. Mill, Bertrand Russell and W.V.O. Quine. Important writers who have made contributions working currently include Donald Davidson, Alvin Goldman, Susan Haack, Jürgen Habermas, Robert Nozick, Richard Rorty and Timothy Williamson.

Information is understandable *data*, data with a meaning.

Information overload is the situation, common in modern society, where someone has everything he or she needs to perform a task, but it is buried in a pile of irrelevant information; the person then may not have the time or resources to find the important stuff. Hence possession of the information is not sufficient for it to be of any use.

The **Internet** is the technological advance that has allowed anyone who can get on to the telephone network and has a suitable receiving system (e.g., a computer, a mobile phone) to access any of billions of computer data files. The relevant technologies are very simple: TCP/IP and dynamic routing. The net effect – no pun intended – is to bring the largest quantity of information ever gathered together within everyone's reach.

Know-how is a type of knowledge often ignored by epistemologists, yet is (a) a very common type of knowledge, and (b) extremely import-ant as far as the knowledge economy goes. Representing know-how, rather than propositional knowledge, is one of the most imperative tasks of the version of *epistemology* outlined in this essay. In the knowledge-management literature, the terms used for know-how and propositional knowledge are *procedural knowledge* and *declarative knowledge* respectively.

Knowledge is a type of *information* that aids the performance of effective actions. Traditionally, *epistemologists* have focused on the psychological aspects of knowledge; however, modern conditions – the *knowledge economy* – have shown the need to expand the definition of knowledge to include non-psychological states.

Knowledge acquisition is the process of adding knowledge to an agent's stock (the agent can be human, or non-human such as an organisation). Tasks for a reconstructed *epistemology* include: outlining reliable methods for acquiring knowledge from people, computers and economic markets; and finding ways of discovering knowledge that exists only implicitly within an organisation and making it explicit.

The **knowledge economy** is one in which knowledge is a force of production and a source of competitive advantage. The exploitation of raw materials and labour characterised the so-called old economy; the knowledge economy involves a general switch to services from manufacturing, and places a premium on an educated and productive workforce.

Knowledge management is the task of making sure that an organisation's consumption, acquisition and use of knowledge is cost-effective. In other words, the task of: ensuring that any knowledge that the organisation possesses is used as often and efficiently as possible; ensuring that any knowledge that the organisation needs but does not possess is acquired; ensuring that all the knowledge the organisation possesses adds as much as possible to the organisation's effectiveness.

Knowledge sharing is a tricky part of *knowledge management*. Within an organisation, particularly a big or widely spread one, it is often the case that the knowledge that organisation possesses does not get to the people who need it. Employee X does not know that employee Y knows how to solve X's current problem. The aim of knowledge sharing is to ensure that X can find out who in the organisation can help him or her, without contributing too much to *information overload*.

Scepticism is a type of philosophical objection to a theory, objecting to the basic assumptions of that theory. Sceptical arguments are usually very pernicious, and the net result of *epistemological* scepticism has been that, over the millennia, epistemologists have spent much too much effort trying to confound the sceptic and not enough finding out about knowledge, and therefore modern-day epistemology is not adequate for the serious epistemological problems of *knowledge management* and the *knowledge economy*.

The **Semantic Web** is a development of the *World Wide Web*, involving the use of the markup language XML which allows a Webpage to include within it a specification of the knowledge it contains. This will allow much more intelligent searching and navigation of the Web.

The **World Wide Web** is a portion of the *Internet* which provides a common format for multimedia computer files to be displayed on-screen through a browser. It exploits the markup language HTML, which governs the display of data on-screen, and is not tied to any one operating system (such as Windows or Linux). This gives the Web a common look and feel, wherever you are accessing it from.

Heidegger, Habermas and the Mobile Phone

George Myerson

'It Was Good To Talk': Mobile Phones and German Philosophers

'If you want to keep pace with the changing environment . . . the global economy of the day, you need a fast means of communications,' says Tansa Musa.
'Front Page World', www.bbc.news.co.uk, 4 September 2000

The BBC has just asked a citizen of Cameroon to explain what it calls 'mobile phone frenzy' which is 'hitting' the country. The answer is twofold. Mobiles are practical, they have their uses. But beyond the practicality, the mobile is the object which most closely embodies the spirit of the 'changing environment'. If you want to assure yourself that you belong to the new century, this is the object to have in your hands – unless it's a 'hands-free'. Musa's brilliantly concise response points towards a big question: *how* has the once anodyne 'telephone' become the new must-have mobile?

At the moment, as the new millennium starts, we are witnessing, and being addressed by, a ubiquitous campaign to promote the mobile phone. This mobile propaganda is extraordinary in its energy, its resources and its cultural impact. There are the old-style ads, but there is also a torrent of information released through diverse media, on the web, via other products and sales outlets. You can hardly tune in to a major sporting event without finding the logo of a mobile company featured either among the competitors or over the occasion as a whole.

The promotion is twofold: its subject is first of all a whole new technology, and then an individual brand. This doubleness must pose interesting dilemmas for publicists of the individual corporations: can you promote your brand specifically or are you really just promoting the whole technology? There is plenty to say about the mobile campaign. You can deconstruct the images, as with all such publicity. You can find stereotypes and ideological undercurrents. But in this 'postmodern encounter', I propose to look at this mobile hubbub from a more surprising perspective: an alien perspective.

Our encounter will be between this new mobile culture and two leading thinkers of the 20th century: Martin Heidegger and Jürgen Habermas. (See 'Appendix' for brief profiles.) In his great work, *Being and Time* (1927), Heidegger initiated one of the most important 20th-century discussions of talk or, as he also called it, 'discourse'. These ideas were taken up, criticised and developed in different ways by many European and American thinkers, notably among German philosophers of communication, of whom the latest representative is Jürgen Habermas, whose *Theory of Communicative Action* (1981) has shaped two decades of debate about dialogue and modern society. The nub of this encounter is the idea of communication itself, for, in their different ways, both the 20th-century philosophers and the 21st-century mobile persuaders claim to be redefining what it means for human beings to communicate.

What makes this encounter a postmodern one? In architecture especially, 'postmodern' often means the mixing of old and new, futuristic and archaic styles. This encounter is postmodern in that architectural sense: here the old thinkers come together with the new cultural wizards. Apart from striking sparks off one another, these contrasting perspectives also reveal – as they collide – something significant about the break between the old and the new centuries. Both the philosophers and the mobile campaigners are interested not just in routine communication, but in the road to utopia. For all their differences, the two 'discourses' share the view that modern utopia will be about ideal communication.

The 'Great Mobilisation' of the Year 2000: 'It's great to communicate.'

'Well, my friends, think of the old Che Guevara poster you once

had on your bedroom wall. This is a popular uprising, carried out by mobile phone . . .'

Leandra de Lisle, 'My friends on the barricades',
www.guardianunlimited.co.uk, 13 September 2000

How many meanings this new telephone can carry! Symbol of the new global economy one minute, the very next minute the mobile is an emblem of the new revolution. It seems as if this magic thing can release the hidden power latent in the ordinary process of communication. By the magic of the mobile, a few truck drivers and farmers are transformed into a 'petrol blockade' of Britain to rival the Second World War. Even in such news items, the march of the mobile campaign goes on, fuelled – unlike everything else – by protest and picketing as much as by Internet and e-commerce.

Anything as massive as the mobile campaign most certainly deserves its own name, and clips like this glimpse of the new 'barricades' suggest one: MOBILISATION. Alongside its martial connotations, the word also has useful echoes of 'globalisation', the catchphrase of the new century. Mobilisation is a way of connecting what Tansa Musa in Cameroon says about the new telephone in the 'global economy' and what Leandra de Lisle writes about the new outlaws and their modern-day smoke-signals. What is being 'mobilised' in all the imagery and persuasion, the catchphrasing and informing? In the first place, however obvious it might sound, what is occurring is the mobilisation of that old telephone. The mobilisation of the phone isn't really a technological process – it's cultural. The problem isn't to *invent* a machine, but to get us all to *adopt* it, to feel we need it. Because, of course, it's we that need to be mobilised.

Let's look briefly at the ingredients of mobilisation. The classic British Telecom telephone slogan of the last century was: 'It's good to talk . . .'. That is really a pre-mobilisation slogan. Something radical has happened since that now nostalgic time. Talk is still an important theme in the massive cultural text that is being woven around the mobile. But, especially in the more 'informative' presentations, you have dizzying images of talking all around, a feeling that does perhaps match our everyday experience of the onset of the mobile era. Instead of the old-style 'conversation', you have the multiplication of talk:

[T]*he number of cellular phones in this country* [is estimated] *to be near 77 million, with more than 37,500 people signing up for wireless phone service each day. And these users are talking more than ever before.* . . . [T]*here is too much traffic on the phone network* . . . [My emphasis.]

New York Times, 19 August 2000

In this clip, you find the key ingredients of the new mobilisation. First come the numbers; the new promotion of the mobile is all about numbers – and they are staggering. So many people are signing up per second, so many people will be on the mobile by next week, next month, next year. Second, there is the sense of what James Gleick calls 'acceleration'. You could no longer say that 'it's good to talk'; the message is much more zappy, more like: 'It's great to communicate!'

The old familiar telephone has become part of something else, *that* is the message, and in the process there has been an explosion of energy, an immense interconnection. Old slow-moving 'talk' is being rapidly pushed aside by its faster cousin 'communication'. You can feel that pressure in the little warning note: all that talk is making the traffic move too slowly, a kind of communicative gridlock is setting in. We will need, the implication is, some better way to communicate in the future. The destiny of the mobile is to take us beyond the 'world of talk', into some other world where 'communication' means something far richer and also far quicker.

The phone is an object and a technology. But it is also part of a system of ideas, even a way of looking at everyday life. The phone has become part of an idea of the family, of intimacy, emergency and work. The message of mobilisation is that the old phone is no more, and so that old system of ideas has also passed away. You may assume that you know what a phone is and does, what it is for. But the essence of the language of mobile promotion is to show that you don't yet understand your phone. You are stuck in the last century, until you have 'got' mobilisation. Talk is the starting point in understanding this new-style object, but soon the talking stops:

It's perfectly **suited to talking to people,** *to receiving short messages, screening short movie clips, holding video conferences on the move, receiving headlines.* [My emphasis.]

Orange Press Release, 13 July 2000

Yes, of course the mobile is about talking, but already they have to add 'to people' – an important phrase. You can no longer assume that people are on the receiving end of this 'talk'. Now talk is part of a web of uses – and here the phone is being redefined, and with it human communication. Again, there is a tremendous sense of multiplication, this time the multiplication of *functions* of your phone. Yes, it's good to talk, but look at all the other ways of communicating down the line.

And so there arises the possibility of this new advice:

The Person You Are With is the **Most Important Person To Talk To.** [My emphasis.]

Nokia Press Release, 12 July 2000

You can see here just how far talk itself is being re-made and even overtaken in the project of the mobile phone as it enters the 21st century. 'Talk' stands for an old sense of person-to-person presence and contact. The new phone mobilisers show you they aren't against such traditions, on the contrary. At the same time, you can see how this old sense of contact is being surrounded, new meanings pushing it aside. In Nokia's etiquette, there is a vivid picture of what the world must be like, before such advice is needed. The 'You' of this exhortation is being besieged by other voices, by rival message systems.

The philosopher Heidegger might well have agreed with Nokia about its general principle. He devoted a lot of time to the idea of 'being-with', and he certainly saw talking as part of our way to be with others. For Heidegger, in 1927, it was in such moments of contact that a way to be human emerged: 'Man shows himself as the entity which talks.'[1]

Heidegger meant even more than that it was just 'good to talk'. In his philosophy, the message was more like: 'It's human to talk.' For Heidegger, talking was the fundamental activity by which people expressed their experience of 'being-with' each other. From Heidegger's perspective, Nokia's principle is a basic truth, but there is something alarming about the need to remind everyone about it.

That preliminary encounter between Nokia and Heidegger suggests both an overlap and an antithesis. You could say that this is the development which the old philosophers 'asked for', when they made such a to-do about talk and communication! Are we on the threshold of the age when the essential vision of the communication-philosophy is going to become part of our everyday living? Or is the new age going to take 'communication' into territories undreamt of in the last century?

The Age of Communication: Universal Contact

One of the central statements of German communication philosophy was made by the philosopher Karl Jaspers soon after Heidegger had presented his ideas about being human: '[P]hilosophic truth sees all human beings as possible others with whom it remains our task to communicate.'[2]

Jaspers was writing in 1932, on the eve of Hitler; unlike Heidegger, he was a consistent anti-fascist. Taking off, nevertheless, from Heidegger's ideas about talking and being, he gives an extraordinary vision of the human condition. For Jaspers, it is our duty as human beings to communicate with all the others. There is no way of fulfilling this duty, and no way of compromising on it. If you think you possess the truth, then you can't stop short in the task of communication. In fact, if you take your ideas and beliefs at all seriously, then this is your duty. The idea follows directly from Heidegger on talking and being human, but it has a more obviously progressive spin.

So, one might say, has not the time of this universal communication at last arrived? Poor old Jaspers in 1932, what means of communication did he have at his limited disposal? Pens, type, print, and the old immobile phone. You'd be lucky to communicate with a few thousand people in such a pre-modern condition. If only he could have tuned in to the Nokia website, might he not have found much-needed encouragement to think that his task might be fulfilled in the future? Surely now, humanity can at last achieve what the old philosophers desired, and 'be-with' itself across the globe?

Here is a selection from the Nokia Press Releases Archive for January–July 2000.

10 February: new network to Thailand
3 March: new technology for Japan telecom
29 March: new technology for US apartments
4 April: network in Poland
5 April: technology trial in Hong Kong
12 April: new award in New Zealand
12 April: new networks in Germany
5 May: new joint factory opened by Hungarian and Finnish leaders
8 May: partnership in Israel
11 May: WAP to UK
11 May: advanced trials in Australia
15 May: network advance for Maroc telecom
18 May: commercial network in Norway

22 May: networks in Taiwan
26 May: network to Bolivia
6 June: new digital terminal for Asian market
8 June: WAP solution for Ukraine
14 June: new system in Greece
16 June: WAP networks in China
26 June: network for Finland
26 June: trials in Singapore of new technology
5 July: equipment to Estonia
5 July: network in Denmark
7 July: new data call in Philippines
10 July: network for Austria
11 July: broadband access in France
14 July: 'supply solution' in Belgium

This kind of list is at the core of mobilisation, with its sense of scale and accelerated pace. This archive proclaims the coming of the age when 'mobilisation' will take over from 'globalisation' as the motto on the flag. Now 'all human beings' truly are 'possible others' and we really can, it seems, undertake our moral 'task' and 'communicate with' them, every one of them.

Network after network: you can almost *see* the globe being encircled in a fine mesh of little connecting links. In the mobile vista, communication is on the verge of becoming truly a universal. One could call the outlook 'universal communication', and it is the philosophy implicit in mobilisation as a whole. Of course, such a philosophy fits in with other developments in our time, economic developments that have gone under the heading of 'globalisation'. But it still all sounds like the triumph of the communicative principle, as envisaged by Jaspers and Heidegger in the 1920s and 30s.

It may sound odd to credit mobile phone promotion with a philosophy. Yet this is more than an ordinary, familiar marketing campaign, though it is that as well, of course. The vision runs across official reports and expert statements, as well as ads and one-liners. Highlights across diverse media and institutions show the outlook unfolding. Here it is in 'bureaucrat-ese':

1.1 Their use has escalated over the past decade and to many they are now an essential part of business, commerce and society. Over the Christmas 1999 period alone approximately 4 million phones were sold in the UK and at present (April 2000) there are about 25 million mobile phones in circulation. This is equivalent to nearly one phone for every two people.

'The Stewart Report', independent expert group on mobile phones, May 2000

Staid it may sound, but there is the same communication euphoria as on the commercial websites, the same sense of acceleration, and universality in the wings. This is how humanity is going to find itself, in the new era. Here is the British broadsheet press. In its electronic form, the vision is as follows:

Evidence of Britain's insatiable appetite for mobile phone technology emerged yesterday as figures showed that more than half the population has a mobile. The latest quarterly results showed that network operators had more than 30 million subscribers.

'Half of Britain on the Mobile', www.guardianunlimited.co.uk, 6 July 2000

The key phrase here is 'more than half the population': what happened to the others? It is as if they had failed to register their presence in the world. Next the televised version:

It is believed 3.5 million people bought mobile phones between April and June – an 85% increase on the same period last year.

www.ITN.co.uk, 17 July 2000

And here it is in the US heavyweight press:

According to the ARC Group, a London consulting firm, about 100 million of the world's 500 million mobile phones in use by year-end will be capable of Internet access. Within three years, ARC says, an estimated 300 million of 900 million wireless phones will be Internet ready. Other industry forecasts say that in five years, as many as 500 million people worldwide – one of every dozen – will have phones or other devices capable of wireless Internet access.

New York Times, 10 July 2000

This last highlight adds many of the other key ingredients that make mobilisation distinct and different: it's not just people that are becoming interconnected, but technologies, systems. Surely, when you multiply the web by the mobile, you get universal interconnection? And is not this the destiny of communication, as anticipated by those old German philosophers?

For all the tempting links, the German philosophers would probably not endorse 'mobilisation', even though the two do have in common an immense emphasis on communication as *the* human activity. In the remaining sections, we shall look at the key ingredients in the mobile view of communication, and compare them with their philosophical equivalents. The result is a genuine 'close encounter', and also a striking cultural contrast.

What is 'Communication'? I and We

[T]*he whole concept of communication is being changed.*

Orange Press Release, 13 July 2000

First, let us take the mobilising of communication. Here we begin with the premise that does link the mobile campaign to modern philosophy: communication is a *concept*. There are different versions of this concept, and the mobile campaign is based on the idea that it is possible to change the whole meaning of communication itself. But what is the new concept of communication being adopted and endorsed by the mobile campaign?

Today, wireless phones provide more than 94 million, or one in every three people in the US, with the freedom to communicate – whenever they want, wherever they want.

Nokia Press Release, 12 July 2000

There are two key ideas: first, the sheer scale of interconnection; and second, by contrast, an idea of individual freedom. To be able to communicate is a basic aspect of being free. Indeed, the fact of communication is a key sign of being free. The whole tone of the distinctive mobile concept, however, is established by the recurrent 'they want'. In its mobilised version, communication is all about the fulfilment of an individual *desire* – a want. Being free to communicate is an aspect of getting what you want as much as possible.

There is another way of putting this, which involves ideas other than freedom:

[The new mobilised technology] *should help you take control of the way you communicate* . . .

'The Orange Way', www.orange.co.uk, 18 July 2000

At heart, the mobile concept is about being in control – as a separate and distinct individual. This is the basis of mobilising the concept of communication – that it's an activity undertaken by an individual, over which that individual seeks control. Being in control of communication means being the master of technology itself:

[The new phone-device] *becomes literally your personal communications centre* . . .

Orange Press Release, 13 July 2000

The really striking idea is 'personal . . . centre'. This is a fundamental principle of the mobilisation of communication:
Communication is, at heart, a solitary action. You have your own
communications centre. So we arrive at a major bit of advice,
embodying the basic practice of mobilisation. *Communication
works best when there is only one person involved:*

[I]*t's cheaper than a phone call and doesn't require real-time avail-
ability of the two persons communicating, it's asynchronous . . .*
                                New York Times, 14 March 2000

A postmodern paradox! On the one hand, we have a language
of scale; on the other hand, we have the separate individual
seeking goals. This paradox creates the atmosphere of mobilisation. Countless – but counted – individuals are seeking their
desires separately, and yet unknowingly they are caught up in a
huge system.

Now turn to the slow world of the German philosophers as
they try to redefine the concept of communication. The contrast
is touching, even heart-rending. This is Heidegger:

*Discourse which expresses itself is **communication**. Its tendency
of Being is aimed at **bringing the hearer to participate in dis-
closed Being towards what is talked about in the discourse**.*[3]

The argument moves so slowly over the ground, trying to pin
down the concept of communication which now moves so
quickly. 'Communication' starts from 'discourse', from the
language itself, endowed with a life of its own. This language
seeks to be expressed, and when people give expression to it,
then you have true communication. Heidegger's thinking is,
therefore, right at the other extreme from the mobilised view.
In Heidegger's approach, you could not look at communication
in terms of an individual speaker wanting control. If there is
a key individual in his definition, it's the hearer, not the

speaker at all. Communication is all about the hearer's understanding. And what Heidegger means is that the hearer should have an experience of the subject being discussed which amounts to a sharing with the speaker. So to try to take control would be a violation of the whole nature of true communication. And the idea of a personal communications centre would be entirely self-contradictory! So too would the emphasis on massive numbers: communication has this personal contact at its heart.

Heidegger's idea evolves into Habermas's concept of 'communicative action'. Here too, there is a contrast with mobilised communication. You can't see communicative action as one person fulfilling an intention. The key to true communication, for Habermas, is 'understanding'. His communicative action is *the use of language with an orientation to reaching understanding*. Communicative action is shared action:

Reaching understanding is considered to be a process of reaching agreement among speaking and acting subjects.[4]

You only have this communication when there is a process by which people come to an understanding about something. And Habermas works out a contrast with what he calls 'instrumental' action or strategy, which is all about taking personal control and fulfilling personal goals.

Orientation to Success versus Orientation to reaching Understanding . . . [I]dentifying strategic and communicative action as types.[5]

If mobilisation were completed, the prime example of communication would not be *two people* – it would be *one* person, set in the context of millions of other separate people. Not that two-person contact would be denied, but it would be secondary. Whereas in the philosopher's tradition, the prime idea has to be two-person contact – or small group engagement.

So the issue isn't whether such a philosopher could or should use a mobile – why not? What's at stake is how to define the *act* of communication itself. From the philosophers' perspective, the mobile campaign is founded on a paradox every bit as mysterious as mysticism, and far less appealing. It would be easier for Heidegger and Habermas to imagine one hand clapping than one person communicating – yet that is the core of the mobile concept.

Why Communicate? Saying What you Want

Mobilisation is a coherent approach not only to marketing a device, but also to living a life. There are answers to all the big questions about communication which troubled the philosophers. For example, why do people communicate? In the mobile outlook, there can be only one plausible explanation: *The Principle of Want.*

This doesn't mean that people 'want' to communicate. That's one of the strangest things about the mobile vision. On the contrary, people communicate in order to satisfy *other* wants. The mobile is the key to satisfying your wants generally. It gets you things. The result is some extraordinary pictures of a new everyday life:

[The mega-advanced communication device will become] *perhaps as small as a stud in your ear . . . eventually you will simply say **what you want** whenever you want it and wherever you want it.* [My emphasis.]

Orange Press Release, 13 July 2000

Here is the key definition: you communicate in order to 'say what you want'. This does not mean what you *mean to say* – it means what you *have to have*.

'Walk down the street, a few blocks away from your favorite

Starbucks, pull out your Web-connected cell phone, you get a
Starbucks menu, click espresso, and it's sent. And you've not
only ordered it, but you've paid and you can go and pick it up.'
New York Times, 2 March 2000

By contrast, Habermas, taking on the spirit of Heidegger, has a
different view of the relationship between want and communication. Again, the difference in texture is important – his is such
a slow argument, definition by definition. But it is all about saying what you want:

We even call someone rational if he **makes known a desire or**
intention, *expresses a feeling or a mood, . . . and* **is then able to**
reassure critics *in regard to the revealed experience by drawing*
practical consequences from it and behaving consistently there-
after.[6] [My emphasis.]

For Habermas, you communicate not in order to satisfy your
desire, but crucially in order to *'make known a desire or inten-*
tion'. You don't aim to satisfy the want by talking; you aim to
disclose it. Then others can respond – that is the suggestion.
They can decide, react, help, hinder. To communicate means to
make your desires understood, not to pursue their immediate
fulfilment.

Now you may say, that's a cumbersome way to think about
going to Starbucks. But Habermas doesn't want to take the visit
to Starbucks as the epitome of human communication. He
wants, on the contrary, to insist that the essential nature of communication is hardly present at all on such occasions or encounters. Habermas's whole philosophy of communication derives
from this distinction between pursuing a goal and seeking to
communicate. Of course, we use words often to satisfy a want,
but for Habermas that isn't true communication. We only actually communicate when we are primarily concerned with making ourselves understood.

In the mobile vision, we have millions of goal-seeking atoms, making basic contacts through the power of the network. In the philosophers' version, you have the slow, distinct 'conversation' through which parties seek a deeper contact . . .

Who Communicates? Device and Voice

We have yet to see, however, just how radical the mobile approach can become. The mobilisation campaign delivers some surprising answers to this basic question: 'Who communicates?'. We have long known from media studies that 'the medium is the message', when it comes to modern communications. But the phone? Here, though, is one answer to 'who communicates?': *Devices.*

*. . . a model to reflect **communications between inanimate objects**, to receive payment for value-added services, as well as charging for conventional voice and data traffic . . .* [My emphasis.]

Orange Press Release, 13 July 2000

Here the company is proposing a new pricing initiative, but as part of that proposition it has to redefine the nature of communication itself, and it does so in this extraordinary way. You might have thought that the meaning of 'inanimate' was precisely 'not able to communicate or be communicated with'. But the language is emphatic, and deliberately reinforces the paradox for rhetorical effect. These are not merely objects, but inanimate objects. Yet they – communications devices and their systems – will be fully recognised as agents of communication. What, then, does the process of communication mean? A touching footnote, for the more traditionally minded, is provided by the acknowledgement of 'conventional voice' as another possible medium. But even then, 'voice' is subsumed with 'data' and both merge with 'traffic' into the flow of the system itself.

In short, this is a language in which communication has no

human agents at all. It is simply a flow of messages, registered in terms of a financial cost. So you check into the system in pursuit of individual desires or aims, and that's the nature of your individual participation. From there, individual agency is swept aside by the sheer flow of traffic through the system.

Another similar plan speaks of:

. . . accelerating the convergence of all communications devices . . .
Orange Press Release, 13 July 2000

As the devices converge, they will be more and more compatible, better and better able to read one another's messages. Now, clearly, there are all kinds of practical positives – I don't mean to offer a Luddite objection to the technology itself. But I do think it is important to notice what this immensely powerful campaign is doing to the concept of communication – what kind of revolution is being enacted with regard to that fundamental 20th-century idea.

Let's turn back, then, to the old century and see how its philosophers struggled to make their revolution in the concept of communication. Habermas recognised that there are many ways in which a modern society needs to economise on communication. After all, his own theory – like Heidegger's – involves a deep recognition of just how much is involved in authentic human communication. Habermas calls the alternative ways of organising people 'systems'. A system is any way of connecting people up, 'going through' the process of reaching understandings among them, that is, communication. Many human arrangements will have to be made by systems rather than by genuine communication. Some of these systems are as basic as money itself, or bureaucratic procedures, or even sheer power:

[R]*elief mechanisms emerge in the form of* **communication media** *that either condense or* **replace mutual understanding in language.**[7] [My emphasis.]

157

No modern society can operate by full-scale dialogue all the time, or even much of the time. You could not run a social security system, or even an education system, like that. All kinds of arrangements get made by substitutes for dialogue – by rules, by the exchange of money or status, by the circulation of impersonal messages. These are 'relief mechanisms', and in a healthy society they would serve to make better spaces in which genuine communication could occur. If communication has to bear the weight of all arrangements, then it will simply collapse under the pressure.

But Habermas foresaw a danger. In the old 20th-century way of such philosophy, he defined that danger as the loss of human texture to parts of our lives: 'The Uncoupling of System and Lifeworld . . .'.[8] By this he meant that the systems would more and more take on a life of their own. The 'lifeworld' is that shared sense of the significance of human actions and experiences, without which the individual is left stranded and searching in isolation for a human meaning to their life. If systems came loose from lifeworlds, then more and more of our lives would be lived according to patterns that had no human significance for us. We would be carrying out tasks without having experiences. And each of us would be living alone. We would feel less and less engaged in our humanity by the institutions and procedures of our society. We would spend our time conforming to rules, rather than engaging in genuine dialogue. And we would find areas of our lives that should depend on dialogue being run as if they were, say, social security systems or bureaucracy. The effect then is that the systems become ever more complicated, as they have to manage more and more of life:

*The more consensus formation in language is relieved by media, the more complex becomes the **network of media-steered interaction**.*[9] [My emphasis.]

As people hand over their lives to be shaped by money or the rules of the power game inside their company or even their family, less and less of life is explored through the dialogue in which one seeks to be understood by others, and to understand them in return. I think most people who were in professions in the late 20th century would be able to make sense of this scenario. Certainly it would be a pretty accurate depiction of life in the British universities of that period, as well as for many working in the health services and other social institutions.

Where once there was communication, now there arise systems:

[A] *heightening of systemic complexity* . . . *unleashes system imperatives that burst the capacity of the lifeworld* . . .[10] [My emphasis.]

This is Habermas's way of saying that we will act increasingly as if we had no freedom to judge, or debate, or even to think. We will feel as if we had no choice. Without communication, there can be no true sense of free choice. The system will drive understanding into the corners of life, and instead substitute procedures to be followed. What counts as reasonable behaviour will then be simply what corresponds to these rules or expectations, these 'imperatives'. Communicative dialogue creates alternatives to explore; systems delete alternatives, and substitute demands.

But the rhetoric of mobilisation would brush aside Habermas's painstaking and heartfelt distinction. The division between system and communication now looks quaint, archaic, a nostalgia for a lost age of leisured inefficiency. What Habermas foresaw as constraint, the mobilisers offer as a liberation. Now the system will do our communication for us.

Just register your desires as swiftly as possible. Then messages will flow to and fro without our needing to engage directly, and that will then be the central meaning of communication. In other words, in the age of full mobilisation, communication would refer primarily to a flow across a system. Voices, and such like, would be simply one small aspect of this traffic. The result, from the perspective of the philosophers, would be the takeover of the term 'communication' by its opposite, the term 'system'.

It's worth returning to Habermas to see just how seriously he might take such a development. He notes already in the latter 20th century 'an extensive uncoupling of system integration and social integration'.[11] 'Integration' is coherence among a group, or even a whole society. Habermas contrasts 'system integration', where people are glued together by common procedures and rules, with 'social integration', where people stay together through a common understanding that they keep working out among themselves. Heidegger too would have understood Habermas's alarm at the rise of 'system integration', whatever their other differences.

In modern life, more and more connections between and among people are made through systems: we are allocated places and times, roles and prospects by means other than dialogue. The university examination process itself is devolving from the old 'viva' tradition to multiple-choice coded assessment programmes. But most importantly, democracy is at stake:

[I]*t is not a matter of indifference to a society whether and to what extent forms of social integration dependent on consensus are repressed and replaced by* **anonymous forms of system-integrative sociation**.[12] [My emphasis.]

The language is cumbersome and makes the argument frustrating to follow. But Habermas isn't being obscure for its own sake. He is trying, perhaps half-successfully, to be precise about a basic distinction between two kinds of social organisation. He is even telling a story in which systems are taking over the role of making people into a 'society' ('sociation'), and communication is being actively 'repressed'. In future, if he is right, people will co-operate because they are each independently following the demands of a system. In a truly communicative society, they would have reached a genuine understanding or 'consensus'. But if you adopted a mobile concept of communication, there would be no difference between system and society, between uniform procedures and genuine consensus.

This is the heart of the matter: is communication simply one function performed by systems, or is it the human pursuit of common understandings? If the mobile concept of communication becomes the norm, that kind of question will feel nostalgic, a remnant of an earlier age. Doesn't it already feel just a little bit quaint, even sentimental?

What is Communicated? Message or Meaning

We have already touched on the next crucial aspect of the mobile redefinition of communication. There's *who* communicates, and then there's *what* is communicated. Here too, the contrast with the philosophers demonstrates just how radical is the new model. In the rhetoric of mobilisation, dialogue is pushed aside by the term 'exchange'.

It's not a coincidence, I think, that this is more often encountered as a financial term. Of course, we have always talked about 'heated exchanges' and so on, but that's different from taking 'exchange' to be the central description of the process by which people communicate. What, then, is being exchanged? The answer is almost always: a message. Here is an amazing example from the everyday life of a phone executive, as celebrated in the *New York Times*:

[He] *spent most of last Thursday in a meeting . . . 'During that time,' he said, 'I exchanged more than 20 messages with my assistant, who was working in another part of the building, confirming appointments and answering questions.' 'Most of the other participants sent and received messages too . . .'*

New York Times, 14 March 2000

Maybe this is OK as a slightly lurid account of an exceptional person at work, but that's not what is meant. This is the prototype of all our lives, and especially all our working lives!

We will live amidst a tidal flow of messages, coming and going, often registered by our communication 'device' on its own. Here you have the peculiar fusion of opposites that makes the mobile vision of the world. On the one hand, you have the supremely individualistic view, you might almost call it atomistic. There's no real gathering at all. Instead, there are only isolated individuals, each locked in his or her own world, making contact sporadically and for purely functional purposes. On the other hand, there is the system of messages, and at that level there are no human agents at all, because they are overwhelmed by the sheer exuberance of the messages as they multiply and reproduce with a life all of their own. Instead of a group, there is on one level just the individual, and on another level just the pure system, servicing itself as effectively as possible.

The exchange model spreads quickly:

[M]*obile devices will play a paramount role in the future of computing and information exchange* . . .

Nokia Press Release, 28 June 2000

Here we see 'device' replacing 'phone' in an increasingly typical way. The effect is to lay down a grid: communication is exchange and exchange is about information, an aspect of data processing. So the exemplary act of communication is an exchange between devices involving the passing over of information content. Here is an extreme case of 'exchange' communication:

When the shelling and gunfire let up, they send a barrage of scathing insults to Manila's forces by cell phone. . . . 'Texting'? Yes, texting – as in exchanging short typed messages over a cell phone. New York Times, 5 July 2000

Yes, the article itself is mildly satirical. But what is interesting is the continued use of the word 'exchanging', far more interesting than the highlight on 'texting'. There is of course the phrase 'exchange of fire', and this really extends the exchange model of communication in new ways. 'Now it's personal', says the avenging hero in countless thrillers. Communication would be personalised warfare, and its messages would be – to adapt Hobbes's old saying – nasty, brutish and economical.

The question, then, is: what is happening to certain important words, images and ideas? Something very different from what would have happened under the influence of the philosophers. Habermas in particular provides a graphic contrast with the idea of communication as the exchanging of messages. From his perspective, there are some critical ingredients missing. The most important is 'understanding'. As we have seen, he insists that communication must serve 'the *functions of achieving understanding* in language' [my emphasis].[13] The use of 'in language' in this sentence draws attention to another basic idea about communication. For understanding to be achieved in language, you must have something else in common, and that is meaning. For Habermas, to communicate is to engage with meanings, in the hope of achieving a shared understanding of the world.

Messages are very different from meanings. At most you could say that a message is a very narrowed-down model of meaning – a one-dimensional version of meaning. Habermas's philosophy allows us to distinguish clearly between messages and meaningful expressions:

And the rationality of those who participate in this communicative practice is determined by whether, if necessary, they could **under suitable circumstances, provide reasons for their expressions.**[14] [My emphasis.]

'Rationality' is Habermas's term for the potentiality that people have to act and speak in ways for which they could give reasons. Expressions, therefore, have meaning in so far as the speaker could give reasons for them. This sounds a bit dry, but reasons needn't be dry: 'I said this because I wanted to convey the feeling of . . . ; the argument for . . . ; the experience of . . . ; to evoke the atmosphere of . . . .' A message is an expression without such reasons, really. It has a purpose rather than reasons. I would send a message to get someone to come to my office at noon. Of course, we need such messages, and they have their place in Habermas's schema. But to make such messages definitive for mainstream communication is to exclude most of the possibilities of human expression. It's a black and white universe.

Habermas makes a sharp division between commands and meaningful communication. Commands have their place. But if a society went down the path of organisation by instruction, it would lose touch with 'good reasons':

*. . . as in relation to imperatives – the **potential for the binding (or bonding) force of good reasons** – a potential which is always contained in linguistic communication – remains unexploited.*[15] [My emphasis.]

For Habermas, a society that arranged its affairs by exchanging 20 or 30 messages an hour (in the background) would soon forget what is involved in a meaningful expression – how much can be said, how much should be said. Such a society would be 'pathological':

Such communication pathologies can be conceived of as a result of a confusion between actions oriented to reaching understanding and actions oriented to success.[16]

In the '30-an-hour' message world, success is the aim. You say as little as possible to make sure you get what you want as fast as you can. Fine in some circumstances. But if a whole society took this as the height of good communication, then it would, in Habermas's view, lose touch with the deeper sense of communication which has played a fundamental role in human evolution to this point.

When is Communication Going Well? The Right Response

So we come to the question of 'good communication'. Models of communication are never neutral; each implies an ideal scenario. Here the relationship between the 21st-century mobile concept and the 20th-century philosophical concept is strange. They do converge on an idea: *response*. In both approaches, to communicate well means to arouse a response, to which you in turn respond. But the convergence is deceptive, and it hides a deep conflict, perhaps the deepest of all.

In mobile communication, the ideal is represented by the swiftest possible route to the most direct response:

. . . *taking wireless communication beyond two dimensional voice and data into **intelligent, interactive response** to individual customer requests* . . . [My emphasis.]

Orange Press Release, 13 July 2000

The key words are culturally rich: 'intelligent', 'interactive'. But this latter is also the give-away. This is a 'virtual reality' model of interactivity. The word 'response' seems to suggest a human element. But, in fact, the ideal scenario has only one human in it. The response comes from the *system itself* and not from another person. Here, then, are the two conflicting aspects of the mobile model brought together. You have the desire-seeking individual making contact with the massive system in order to attain the desired fulfilment. In turn, the system behaves as if it were a fellow human agent, except that it is altogether more efficient and 'intelligent':

Imagine walking into Bloomingdale's and simply saying, 'I'll buy this, thank you,' to which a voice responds, 'That will be

$220. Do you confirm?' You then say, 'Yes, I confirm.' The machine says, 'Thank you, have a nice day,' and you walk out the door with your purchase.

New York Times, 2 March 2000

The key phrase is 'a voice responds'. This is the ideal moment. But what a voice, and what response!

Habermas too has 'interaction' and 'response' high on his agenda, but in a different way. Here he really does take the long view, looking right back into the mists of evolution and applying his theories to the behaviour of species like dogs and even simpler organisms! In this theory, communication has evolved from certain very basic interactions where 'response' first occurred:

*The interaction is set up in such a way that the beginnings of movement on the part of one organism are the gestures that serve as **the stimulus eliciting a response** on the part of the other.*[17] [My emphasis.]

Two 'organisms', presumably from the same species, are watching one another. One makes a move, and the second 'responds'. Habermas takes the view that only in the most primitive stages of evolution does the 'response' follow mechanically from the original gesture, without anything resembling 'understanding' coming into play. In other words, 'understanding' begins quite low down on the evolutionary scale, the moment the response involves any kind of processing of the original gesture. What gets added by evolution is understanding – first of the other and then of oneself:

*An advantage accrues to participants **who learn not only to interpret the gestures** of others in the light of their own instinctually anchored reactions, **but even to understand the meaning of their own gestures in the light of the expected responses of others.***[18] [My emphasis.]

Evolution favours those organisms which (or who) respond with insight. Their response follows from a sense of the meaning both of their own gesture and that of the other.

Habermas is clearly talking of pre-verbal gestures: we are in the world of apes, maybe, or even dogs, or perhaps birds on a branch or lizards in the sun. So when you look again at the Bloomingdale's scenario, you get an alarming picture, as if evolution were being thrown backwards, as if under the guise of progress there were an immense degeneration. Meaning is bypassed, as being too slow a medium for the ideal interaction. The aim now is to eliminate understanding altogether, to return to a 'conversation of gestures' more basic even than this early phase that Habermas sketches.

Habermas's evolutionary scheme does not stop there, either. From understanding and responding, we move on to fully rational communication. Now we have the principle of 'communicative rationality': '[B]asing the rationality of an expression on its being **susceptible of criticism** and grounding . . . .'[19] In this phase, it isn't enough to grasp the meaning of what is said. You need to understand the reasons behind it, and its potential weaknesses. At this advanced level, the ideal dialogue looks more like a debate: '[T]he central presupposition of rationality: [expressions] **can be defended against criticism.**'[20] [My emphases.]

Communication is rational only when it has this element of debate, or potential for debate, inside it. Of course, the criticism and defence is usually silent, or implied, or just side-stepped. But it is there in reserve, waiting to be taken up. So you can't claim to understand what someone has said, if you couldn't say why you agree (or disagree): 'We understand a speech act when we know what makes it acceptable.'[21]

From Habermas's point of view, the most disturbing feature of the mobile ideal is that it leaves no space for this criticism at all, and so no scope for achieving true agreement. For you only get a valid agreement on the basis of facing objections or answering questions. In mobile communication, there are no reasons, and no scope for involving them seems to open out. On the contrary: you want what you want, and the voice will comply if you can pay. OK, as an aspect of consumption. But as a model of communication?

You might feel, as I do, that Habermas exaggerates the role of criticism in ideal communication. So you might then turn back to Heidegger for an alternative version of the ideal 'response' with which to assess the mobile scenario. By contrast with the mobile version, Heidegger and Habermas have a lot in common. At the heart is this notion of contact, of response as closeness:

*In the same way, **any answering counter-discourse arises proximally and directly from understanding** what the discourse is about, which is already 'shared' in Being-with.*[22] [My emphasis.]

This has not got Habermas's emphasis on reasons, maybe, but still there is a sense of depth to the connection. There is something *behind* the response. The key is 'understanding', which is the deep-level link between Habermas and Heidegger, a link which is going to mean more and more in the face of the mobile vision.

In the mobile scenario, communication is good when the intelligent response delivers the desired outcome as swiftly as possible. In Heidegger's scenario, communication is good when an answering voice arises not far from the initial utterance, not far in space or time maybe, but more profoundly, *not far* in human understanding. The greater the distance between the answer and the initial voice, the further we are from the ideal. This closeness may not be about agreement. But it is definitely about understanding. Indeed, what Heidegger means by 'understanding' is the closeness of the responding voice to the original. In this argument, 'proximally' means nearby, in touch.

The contrast is really about space and time. For Heidegger,

the metaphor is spatial. The answer arises 'close by' the original. For mobilised communication, the ideal is expressed in terms of time, and the response comes as swiftly as possible after the request, for that is what the first voice utters in this scenario. Habermas keeps Heidegger's ideal of closeness, but he adds more sense of argumentativeness, of difference. Either way, the philosophers' ideal scenario feels slow and even tentative. The answering voice takes its time, feels the way.

For both the mobile campaign and the philosophers, a lot of what passes for ordinary communication is less than ideal, even inadequate. In mobile terms, the responses are often too slow, and perhaps the requests aren't clear enough. In philosophical terms, the responses are too fast, and there isn't enough time given to achieving understanding. Here is the real crunch. Both schools (let's call them that) regard ordinary communication as imperfect, or, more positively, as having the potential to be improved. Mobilisation seeks to improve ordinary communication by giving it new channels, clarifying the real meaning of the message, speeding up the response time, whereas the philosophers want communication to be more gradual, more weighted by the search for understanding. Heidegger gives a twist by adding: 'Only he who already understands can listen.'[23] There is a closeness even before true listening. In other words, most of the time, people are not really listening to one another. Again, there is such a sense of slow closing in, or the difficult process of making true contact.

You could say that both mobile campaign and philosophers are revolutionary in their approach to communication. Both regard normal, accepted communication as inadequate, as not living up to its own potential. So you could see these as rival utopian approaches to communication: competing ideals. Knowledge has much to do with both utopias, for the value of communication is everywhere linked to the value of knowledge.

What Do You Learn From Communication? Information and Understanding

It is often said that we are entering 'the information age'. Until recently, the epitome or symbol of the information age has been the Internet, as an aspect of 'computers'. But now the phone is poised to take over and include the Internet within its empire of communication. It may be that the most influential aspect of mobilisation is going to turn out to be this redefining of the information age, and thus of the future which our society is trying to imagine itself as beginning upon. Here is a key example (with a negative twist in the tail):

[A]*s more phones become programmable and **capable of communicating with the Internet and downloading information**, there will be more opportunities for computer viruses* . . . [My emphasis.]

New York Times, 8 June 2000

This 'communicating' means making a connection, entering into the network. Again, it is the device which is 'capable of communicating', in the new language. The 'other' in the communication is a network, not an agent. Of course, many good things can happen – and I'm quite as likely to use it as anyone else. But that's the point. These good things are going to lend credibility to the language of the campaign which surrounds the mobile phone. It is by no means necessary for the technology and its advantages to be wrapped up in this particular model of communication. There are all sorts of alternatives that one can easily imagine – indeed, you only have to compare the way in which the Internet itself emerged and developed with the ways in which the mobile is now being presented.

If the mobile of the future were not such a genuinely powerful and appealing tool, none of this would really matter. But because the mobile is going to be so important, the way in which ideas are associated with it is also important. As society adopts this technology, it is inevitably going to diffuse the associated ideas, images and ways of thinking. At the moment, those ways of thinking centre on the redefining of communication as a potentiality of the device itself – and with that goes a redefinition of knowledge as 'information', because that is what can be imagined flowing into the device as it communicates. In other words, the potential tragedy is that this most rich of technological developments is being packaged in such an impoverishing vision. And this in turn matters because there are a number of other powerful developments with which it fits – in education, in a view of work and of democracy itself.

Learning is being redefined as part of this new model of communication. To learn now means to have the right information pushed at you as efficiently as possible, and education or training will then fit into the wider vision in which:

[U]*sers can access personal Web pages and configure the services they will get through the phone:* **specific information 'pushed' to them** *at a given time* . . .
New York Times, 14 March 2000

'*Our ultimate aim* . . . *is for anyone, anywhere, anytime to* **get access to highly personalized information** *direct from Reuters.*'
New York Times, 12 January 2000
[My emphases.]

Learning, in this scenario, is a process of making sure the right information comes your way as quickly as possible. So communication comes into play as the process by which this information is posted to the right address and delivered with the least possible delay. Ideally, information would be sent out like a FedEx cargo, under guarantee from the agency, whether school or university, writer or publisher, television channel or newspaper.

The old philosophy of the last century provides the basis for an alternative view of knowledge and communication. Perhaps, more pessimistically, you could say that the old philosophy tells us what will be lost in the redefinition of education and knowledge. Habermas concentrates most on this question, as part of his wider concern with rationality – with the potential which human beings have for doings things in ways for which they can provide good reasons:

> [F]*or rationality has less to do with the possession of knowledge than with how speaking and acting subjects acquire and use knowledge* . . .[24] [My emphasis.]

You could not get a stronger contrast with the model in which information is 'pushed' in a correctly targeted way. Instead, you have the idea of a process in which people actively search for knowledge, as part of the wider process of understanding one another. In the mobile scenario, the more information you acquire, the more efficiently you are learning. But Habermas is concerned with 'how' people gain knowledge and 'how' they use it. In his theory, two people could have gained the same information, but one might have acquired it in far richer and more enabling ways than the other. Specifically, a person who had gained knowledge through genuine dialogue might have a richer understanding than someone who had just got hold of the data as swiftly as possible.

Again, you can see the contrast in terms of rival utopian visions. The mobile utopian vision is about instant access to exactly the right information to suit your immediate needs. It is all about gaining, acquiring as efficiently as possible. By contrast, the philosopher lingers over the process of acquisition, precisely the stage which is minimised by the mobile. Put it this way: Habermas would not see acquiring the maximum information in the minimum time as a good definition of learning. But it is the definition implied by the mobile rhetoric of data-pushing and swift access.

The contrast with Habermas is the more significant because the mobile model fits so conveniently with influential approaches in education, in politics and in the media. We are, for instance, employing assessment schemes which subject teachers to judgement resembling the mobile model, rather than the philosophical alternative. A mobile university would look very different from one based on 'communicative rationality'. A company which trained its staff by pushing information out to them would feel very different from one which kept space for at least some mutual understanding. A state which addressed its citizens on the mobile model would stage very different elections from one which tried to keep open spaces for criticism and new consensus. It seems only too plausible that our election campaigns will involve the more and more accurate 'targeting' of 'information'; that we are entering the era of 'm-politics' and leaving behind the ideal, at least, of a more communicative style of political life.

Turn still further back to Heidegger, and again you can see the roots of what Habermas has been saying, and also get an even stronger contrast with the mobilised view of knowledge. For Heidegger, communication was part of a wider phenomenon which he called 'discourse'. Communication was discourse expressing itself. Discourse itself seemed rather mysterious in that pronouncement. Here we can see that, for Heidegger, discourse is about a kind of knowledge: 'Discourse is the Articulation of Intelligibility.'[25] Discourse is any way in which people give expression to their sense that the world is understandable, that a certain experience of the world can make sense.

For Heidegger, communication is the process by which people share, and encourage, their sense that the world can be comprehended, that their experience can become significant. Without such communication, therefore, people will lose confidence in the possibility of understanding their experience of the world. A person who cannot communicate will also find the world more opaque. A society that does not communicate will not give its members the chance to feel that their experience adds up to any kind of coherent whole. Education, then, in this view would be all about supporting the feeling of 'intelligibility' by opening out lines of communication.

Not that Heidegger ignored information in his approach to either knowledge or communication. Here is his rather elaborate idea:

> 'Communication' in which one makes assertions – *giving inform-ation, for instance* – is a special case of that communication which is grasped in principle existentially. In this more general kind of communication, the Articulation of Being with another is understandingly constituted.[26] [My emphasis.]

What does he mean? In the present context, he means that giving and receiving information should only be taken as a small aspect of the wider process of communication, and wider field of understanding. In Heidegger's terms, the mobile model threatens to make a minor part of communication into the central case. Of course, information is passed across. But that is as part of the wider process in which people seek to share their sense of being.

I suppose, on the whole, the postmodern encounter of the new mobile culture and the old philosophy of communication points towards some pessimistic conclusions. Heidegger and Habermas certainly draw attention to the losses which might be the underside of 21st-century progress. But there is also a hint of an alternative, truly utopian conclusion. The mobile technology is clearly not going to be switched off. It is going to develop in all kinds of new directions. But does that technology need to come packaged in the mobile concept of communication? Could we have the mobile without the mobilisation? Might we, for instance, connect the new technologies of 'information' with the older models of 'how speaking and acting subjects acquire knowledge'? In this utopian glimpse, you might have the mobile technology combined with a richer and more humane sense of what it means to communicate and to learn through communication.

What's the Future of Communication? Value or Money

But that utopian outcome doesn't look likely . . . On the contrary, mobilisation, the whole promotional atmosphere, is turning the mobile technology into a symbol of a certain very narrow vision of modernisation. The mobile is the symbol of the future at the start of the new millennium. And in that symbol, money takes over many areas that in the 20th century had held out against it.

The mobile has, of course, a down-to-earth financial pitch, like any other product being sold:

[A] *simple means of communication that makes financial sense . . .*

'The Orange Way', www.orange.co.uk, 18 July 2000

But even here there is a hint of the deeper significance. Communication is being increasingly measured in terms of money, becoming 'metered'. Of course, some communication always has been done with the meter running. But now metering is going to be a very direct part of everyday contact all the time, at work and beyond. How many resources have been sunk into this five-minute discussion? How much was arranged? How much skill was acquired? How many customers were appeased? The question is whether there will remain, anywhere, a space for communication which does not make financial sense, or is not analogous to financial sense. Will the only test of communication be: how much did it cost?

The prospects are not good for those with a lingering attachment to the old models of dialogue. We are, in the language of mobilisation, only at the beginning of the new era. This object, once a phone and increasingly a 'device', looks set to carry into the 21st century the idea that communication is a sub-set of exchange, and, as such, it will ultimately fall under the rule of money:

For those still fixated with e-commerce, forget it . . . The latest thing is m-commerce, as in mobile phone.
www.guardianunlimited.co.uk, 4 July 2000

This is a moment really worth pausing over. The meaning of 'mobile' is changing here with the introduction of the 'm' in 'm-commerce'. Now the same 'm' will stand for mobile and for money. Ultimately it is money which is destined to be mobilised in the coming century. It may turn out that the mobilisation of talk, of communication, of information, is only a stage on the way to the bigger mobilisation.

The speeding up of exchange is going to be the ruling metaphor in the world of finance, making a:

*Promise to turn your cell phone or handheld organizer into **an electronic wallet**.* [My emphasis.]
New York Times, 2 March 2000

There is a sense of magic, transfiguration, metamorphosis. Objects seem to be on the verge of leading a life of their own. New categories are being born. What will it mean when one object is both your communication device, your organiser and your money supplier? This m-device heralds a new dance. A new conception of everyday life is being sketched, and at the heart of this new conception is the new concept of communication. The mobilising of communication turns out to be the precursor, the necessary precondition, for this larger mobilisation of the everyday. This 'm' stands for a new order of everyday life: faster, neater, sharper.

From the old philosophy, we get a different perspective on a similar future. First, from Habermas, there is the idea that changes in communication will go with a new society. But here the process is seen as ambiguous and often destructive:

The transfer of action co-ordination from language over to steering media . . . such as money and power ... [These media] *encode a purposive-rational attitude . . .*[27] [My emphasis.]

And Habermas had not glimpsed the m-commerce world! This m-future goes much further than the 'transfer' he is imagining. Now we are looking, in the terms of his philosophy, towards a future where communication is incorporated into 'money and power' so thoroughly that it has no separate sphere at all. There will, if the m- is the future, be no idea of communication distinct from the idea of commerce. To communicate will mean the same thing as to exchange money. The two activities will simply be merged.

But for Habermas that merger, or take-over, would be a disaster, and an irreversible one. It is only because the idea of communication remains partly distinct from power and money that there is any place from which to criticise those systems. The mobile here begins to signify the end of philosophy itself, as understood by the tradition running (with many strains and breaks) from Heidegger to Habermas. Their ideas would be swept aside by this new *m-communication*, which would be impermeable to their thinking.

Communication would then become a matter of pure technique. But just think how many places there are where you are offered just such a model of communication! How many opportunities you have, at work, or in your personal life, to acquire better communication skills, as if that were quite independent of any content that you might have to communicate, or anyone you might wish to speak with. If m-communication overcomes communicative action and communication rationality, it will be the end of what this philosophy calls 'the lifeworld' – that is, the world experienced as a lived environment: my world, our world, endowed with my and our meanings, lived from within, layered with our interpretations. We have no sense of identity outside such a world, not personal identity. But there are alternatives to deep identity – most notably lifestyle – and m-communication goes with the triumph of lifestyle over lifeworld.[28]

It may even be the destiny of the mobile to bring about the cultural disaster which Habermas has foreseen, however clumsily he has expressed the vision:

Societal **subsystems** *differentiated out via media of this kind can make themselves* **independent of the lifeworld,** *which gets shunted aside into the system environment.*[29] [My emphasis.]

The mobile would be the supreme medium for turning everything around into a system, driving out the process of reaching understanding, replacing meanings with messages, consensus with instructions and insight with information. In that process, the lifeworld would be 'shunted aside'. We would be left, co-ordinated but not connected, in a shared web of systems for working and consuming, learning and being together. At last there would be 'a technicization of the lifeworld'.

The terminology is unhappy, almost an example of what it is protesting against: the loss of spontaneous understanding. But in his way, Habermas is imagining a world which cannot distinguish between a credit card transaction and a conversation – or a world where the ideal conversation aspires to the condition of a credit card transaction. That would also be a world in which your diary is your wallet: at last your money and your life will be properly interchangeable! Having too many messages to deal with, we will have to settle for a good lifestyle instead of the good life to which philosophers have pointed since classical times.

To adapt Habermas, you could say that the big question is:

how much of the world is to lie outside the lifeworld? If the life-world is the space in which we give our own significance to experience, not as isolated individuals, but in coherent dialogue with others, then there's a strong argument for saying that, for each person, the lifeworld is shrinking. More and more of our life will be lived in a systems space, where efficient and minimal messaging will replace the slow and messy process of dialogue. Two different kinds of example occur to me: one public and one personal.

The public example is from the news, and takes us back to those truckers with their mobile phone revolution whom we met at the start. You could also use your mobile to consult the government's list of closed petrol stations in September 2000. But at the heart of this conflict – and no doubt the others which will take its place before you read this essay – is a wall of silence: there is not even the hint of contact between the actual prot-agonists. Messages are good at setting up the confrontation more quickly and keeping us informed. You can even use your mobile to e-mail (or m-mail) your views to the BBC. In *Middlemarch*, George Eliot wrote of 'the roar that lies on the other side of silence'. Here, perhaps, is the silence that lies on the other side of the roar of messages. Maybe it would still be good to talk, sometimes, even though it is often great to communicate so swiftly. But it seems that no one can risk the messiness of the open-ended dialogue: how can anyone begin talking with *such people* as the other side? Only a swift message in the ear – or on the screen – can 'resolve' this dispute! Yet mysteriously, disputes refuse to vaporise. On the same day as the petrol crisis reaches a climax, there is a report of a mortar attack in Belfast. Surely the time for talking *must* be past? Haven't those people 'got the message' *yet*?

The personal example concerns changes in what the philo-sopher Jacques Derrida has called 'the university space'. When I finish a course now, I hand out a form to students to get 'feed-back'. It sounds good, a democratic process. But then just look at the form. There is a list of bullet points, and boxes to tick. Were you interested: Yes/No, or maybe 1–5? Was it audible? Did it fit the course handbook? And the forms are carefully anonymous, so that there can be no retribution or, presumably, corruption. The result is a tide of numbers: one's interest index is only 2.7 this year for Literary History, though one scored 3.6 for audibility in Modern Tragedy. This stuff might be all right if it were the prelude to a dialogue, but as ever in the fast world of mobilised opinion, this is the substitute for dialogue. The feedback form is born of despair, in its little way, despair at the possibility of ever undertaking actual contact with so many people, and across such absolute divisions of self-interest as must separate the student who is being assessed and the teacher who will do the grading. This too is a roar with a deep silence on the other side.

Ultimately, it is the future that is the subject of this 'postmodern encounter', the future as conceived in terms of communication. At times, the mobile promotion hypes the future like any other advertising, promising:

> . . . *a range of services to take wireless communications into a new dimension* . . .
>
> www.orange.co.uk, 18 July 2000

But at other times, the rhetoric of mobilisation seems to go beyond advertising hype, and intervene in the theory of modern utopias, most notably in such moments as we saw at the beginning:

> *Today, wireless phones provide more than 94 million, or one in every three people in the US, with the freedom to communicate – whenever they want, wherever they want.*
>
> Nokia Press Release, 12 July 2000

That old-fashioned word 'wireless' – which in Britain used to mean the *radio* – has been reborn as the symbol of a new utopian dream of a wireless world, where 'freedom' will mean the power to communicate on your own terms, 'whenever' and 'wherever' *you* choose. It is a powerful vision of the m-future. In this encounter, this m-future has been defining itself in a dialogue with Heidegger, Habermas and the philosophy of authentic communication, from 'talk' and 'discourse' to 'communicative action'. That philosophy of communication is no more finished than the mobile campaign. Will the old philosophy find new alternatives to the m-future? Let's hope we will recover a touch of 's-communication', where 's' stands for 'still'.

Appendix: Brief Background to Heidegger and Habermas

Martin Heidegger

Introduction

Martin Heidegger (1889–1976) was the most important, and also the most controversial, influence on modern European philosophy – often referred to as the 'continental' tradition by contrast with the 'analytic' approach of the Anglo-American school. Heidegger's major work was *Being and Time*, published in 1927. There he gave expression to a philosophical vision of 'man' as a being 'thrown' into the world, and always in search of an 'authentic' identity. Though Heidegger himself soon drew close to German Fascism in the 1930s, these ideas from *Being and Time* reached far wider than his own particular approach, and influenced thinkers from all political, moral and religious quarters throughout the 20th century. Other major developments of Heidegger's thinking are found in 'What is Metaphysics?' (1929) and *Letter on Humanism* (1947).

Being and Time

This 'Postmodern Encounter' draws upon *Being and Time* for Heidegger's views of talk and communication. In that book, Heidegger saw himself as recalling philosophy to 'the question of Being', and developed a complex account of our 'being-in-the-world'. Heidegger believed that Western philosophy had lost touch with the important questions of human existence. Writing in the aftermath of the First World War, he gave an urgent account of human life as a search for its own meaning and identity, unaided by any external authority or fixed values.

Heidegger's treatment of 'talk' and 'discourse' arises as part of his picture of the human search for the significance of our own 'being':

Discoursing or talking is the way in which we articulate 'significantly' the intelligibility of being-in-the-world.[30]

Discourse is broader than talk, including all of our inner and outer expression which plays the same role as talking. No single concept has been more important to modern thought than this idea of discourse.

Talk and Discourse

- Do NOT have the purpose of transmitting messages or information.
- Are NOT ways of getting things we want more efficiently.
- Do NOT give expression to 'me–I'.

- DO have the purpose of finding significance.
- DO have the purpose of sharing understanding.
- DO give expression to human being-in-the-world.

These ideas of communication were taken up by important thinkers, including Karl Jaspers (1883–1969), who in *Philosophy* (1932) argued that only in 'communication' could man 'become himself'. While Heidegger drew closer to the Nazis, Jaspers courageously refused all collaboration and continued to uphold this communicative ideal, which, however, still had deep roots in Heidegger's original ideas of discourse and talk.

Jürgen Habermas

Introduction

Jürgen Habermas has been a leading influence on contemporary thought since the appearance of his monumental two-volume *Theory of Communicative Action* (1981). There, Habermas sees himself as laying 'The Foundations of Social Science in the Theory of Communication'.[31] The direct influences on this theory are sociological theorists, notably Max Weber and Theodor Adorno. Habermas belongs to the tradition of the democratic Left, and has been a notable critic of the inheritances of Fascism in Germany and beyond. But in its core vision, Habermas's work also develops Heidegger's story in which talk has arisen to give expression to the human search for meaning, rather than to convey useful messages. Habermas acknowledges his critical involvement with Heidegger's thought in *The Philosophical Discourse of Modernity* (1987), in which he presents himself as discovering a lost opportunity which his predecessor had overlooked in his own system. The later developments of Habermas's arguments are gathered in his collection entitled *Between Facts and Norms* (1996), in which there is an increasing engagement with the ethical and legal implications of his ideas of communicative action.

The Theory of Communicative Action

Habermas starts with the question: what does it mean to say that a person, or an action, or a way of life, is *rational*? His ultimate aim is to give an account of the evolution of modern society in terms of different ways of being rational, or of becoming *more* rational. For Habermas, to become more modern means to become more rational, which sounds rather optimistic or even complacent. However, he makes a vital distinction between two different ways of being rational. First there is 'instrumental rationality', which is about 'successful self-maintenance' – that is, the effective pursuit of your own interests, the efficient pursuit of your own goals.[32] Then, by contrast, there is 'communicative rationality'.

Communicative Rationality

- Is NOT defined as the competitive pursuit of your own aims and interests.
- Is NOT about devising 'strategies' for success.

- IS about the achievement of shared understandings through language and other means of communication.
- IS about being open to criticism and able to give *good reasons* for your beliefs, decisions and actions.

'Communicative action' is based upon this kind of rational agreement, achieved either through actual dialogue or through other means of achieving shared understanding.

In Habermas's theory, communicative rationality has the 'potential' to create a society which is more modern in the sense of being more open. But he sees the rival, instrumental rationality as being in the ascendant, creating a society which is more modern only in the sense of being more effective at delivering the goals of those in power, or more efficient at servicing the systems of money. Habermas has produced a new way of criticising modern society, in which many values and ideas associated with the political and intellectual Left are combined with an idea of communication that still has deep roots in Heidegger.

Notes

1. *Being and Time*, p. 208.
2. *Basic Philosophical Writings*, p. 76 (*Philosophy*).
3. *Being and Time*, p. 312.
4. *Theory of Communicative Action I*, p. 287
5. Ibid., pp. 286–8.
6. Ibid., p. 15.
7. *Theory of Communicative Action II*, p. 181.
8. Ibid., p. 153.
9. Ibid., p. 184.
10. Ibid., p. 155.
11. Ibid., p. 185.
12. Ibid., p. 186.
13. *Theory of Communicative Action I*, p. 308.
14. Ibid., p. 17.
15. Ibid., p. 305.
16. Ibid., p. 332.
17. *Theory of Communicative Action II*, p. 7.
18. Ibid., p. 12.
19. *Theory of Communicative Action I*, p. 9.
20. Ibid., p. 16.
21. Ibid., p. 297.
22. *Being and Time*, p. 207.
23. Ibid., p. 208.
24. *Theory of Communicative Action I*, p. 8.
25. *Being and Time*, p. 204.
26. Ibid., p. 205.
27. *Theory of Communicative Action II*, p. 183.
28. For the rise of 'lifestyle', see e.g. Anthony Giddens, *Modernity and Self-Identity* (Cambridge: Polity Press, 1991).
29. *Theory of Communicative Action II*, p. 183.
30. *Being and Time*, p. 204.
31. *Theory of Communicative Action II*, p. 3.
32. *Theory of Communicative Action I*, p. 171.

Further Reading

The key texts have been used in the following editions:

Martin Heidegger, *Being and Time*, trans. J. Macquarrie and E. Robinson (Oxford: Blackwell, 1962). For further reading, I recommend: Part V, Sections 31 ('Being-There as Understanding'), 34 ('Being-There and Discourse') and 35 ('Idle Talk').

Jürgen Habermas, *The Theory of Communicative Action I*, trans. T. McCarthy (London: Heinemann, 1984).

Jürgen Habermas, *The Theory of Communicative Action II*, trans. T. McCarthy (Cambridge: Polity, 1984).

The most useful background sources are:

C. Guignon (ed.), *The Cambridge Companion to Heidegger* (Cambridge, UK: Cambridge University Press, 1993).

S.K. White (ed.), *The Cambridge Companion to Habermas* (Cambridge, UK: Cambridge University Press, 1995).

I have also cited:

Karl Jaspers, *Basic Philosophical Writings*, trans. E. Ehrlich, L. Ehrlich and G. Pepper (Humanities Press, 1994).

Other related works include:

Avital Ronell, *The Telephone Book: Technology, Schizophrenia, Electric Speech* (Lincoln: University of Nebraska Press, 1989). This is a deconstructive reflection on Heidegger's theory of conscience as a 'call', using excerpts from his involvement with the Nazi Party as a counterpoint.

Geoff Mulgan, *Connexity: How to Live in a Connected World* (London: Chatto, 1997). A balanced response to the social impacts of new communications.

James Gleick, *Faster* (London: Abacus, 1999). A chronicle of contemporary relationships between new technology and human experience.

Marshall McLuhan and Virtuality

Christopher Horrocks

Introduction: Saint McLuhan

Man, he understood the Internet. He was the Internet in the sixties. The world's just finally caught up to him. He was an internet in the sense he was in touch with the entire globe. . . . He was wired long before the editors of Wired *magazine were born. This man was truly wired.*[1]

Robert Logan

. . . the Christian concept of the mystical body – all men as members of the body of Christ – this becomes technologically a fact under electronic conditions.[2]

Marshall McLuhan

The arrival of the computer-driven information revolution, along with its strange geographies of cyberspace, virtual reality, the Internet and the Web, has for some people reinvigorated the writings and ideas of Marshall McLuhan. For many, his name is synonymous with his phrase 'the medium is the message'.[3] In other words, the content of media is less important than the impact of each medium at social, psychological and sensory levels. McLuhan also introduced the vivid notion of the 'global village', which described the connection of the world by electronic media. He claimed that transmissions by satellite and other relays (Sputnik having circled the Earth in 1957 and turned it into the content of a mediated environment) had transformed society from the mechanical, objective, uninvolved and 'visual' world of print into an electronic one which was immersive, involved, immediate and 'acoustic' (see the Glossary at the end of this essay). McLuhan spoke of a new 'tribal' electronic consciousness that would replace the individuated culture that had dominated the West since the invention of the printing press.

This essay explores the encounter of Marshall McLuhan's major insights into media and technology with the present world of information networks, e-commerce, digital technology and the age of virtual reality. The encounter was one which McLuhan did not live to witness, yet it has been staged under these conditions by those who find a new relevance to his ideas. My brief discussion examines some of the reasons for McLuhan's return, before analysing in more detail the relationship of his main speculations to the current period which I have called 'virtuality' – a broad term which will require some explanation.

Perhaps the most salient example of this liaison between new medium and old messenger is the journal *Wired*, which took the Canadian intellectual as its patron 'saint' of the brave new world of technology, art and communication in 1993. McLuhan's controversial insights were hotly debated and widely disseminated in the 1960s, but to a large extent they were considered marginal and superseded by the time of his death in 1980. However, they now seem appropriate for a medium that arrived just after his message had faded.

McLuhan's legacy for the new generation of academics, journalists and hackers is often phrased as a religious and prophetic one. Paul Levinson said: 'The handwriting for coming to terms with our digital age was on the wall of McLuhan's books.'[4] Others take a more analytical approach to the relationship between McLuhan's canonisation and the religious narratives of his writing. For example, Huyssen elegantly uncovers the theological programme running beneath the McLuhan interface, in which McLuhanist topics such as 'electricity', 'medium' and 'global village' can be replaced by 'Holy Spirit', 'God' and 'Rome' respectively.[5] In a similar manner, Genosko critically inquires whether McLuhan's 'fooling around' was founded on a specific faith, whereby salvation from the fall of literacy might be found in electric technology.[6]

Richard Coyne's philosophical study of new technology makes the link between spiritual values and a romantic sensibility towards our new media.[7] He includes in this scenario McLuhan's proposition that a translation of our entire lives into a spiritual form of information would transform the globe and the 'human family' into a single consciousness.[8] The philosophical and romantic aspects of his work will be explored later.

McLuhan's revival has its problems, and I wish to address these before exploring McLuhan's key thoughts in relation to virtual technology and geography. For example, he has been reprocessed for a new technology and to a certain extent has been sanitised by it, for his explorations are in some cases massaged to provide an affirmative, theoretical slant for the more utopian and idealist discourses of virtuality. As Ostrow remarks, there is no place in the recent, rhapsodic versions of virtual discourses for consideration of McLuhan's belated warning that the impact of the new electronic mass media could be harmful and might need monitoring.[9] Thus, McLuhanism in the new century tends to perpetuate the simplifications of his critics and supporters in the previous one.

It took the Situationist, Guy Debord, whose writing on media and society set him in stark ideological contrast to McLuhan, to make the obvious point that had been ignored by the 1990s McLuhanites: McLuhan's optimism about the potential for freedom and open access of the media had in fact declined by the late 1970s. Debord had identified what he called the 'society of the spectacle', defined as a social relation among people, mediated by images. Capitalistic domination had reached a stage where it could alienate, subjugate and dominate not just through the workplace, but through commodity culture in all its variations, including television and shopping. This theme would later be developed in the work of Jean Baudrillard, whose writing on 'simulation' – the production of social reality through 'codes' such as the mass media – took the concept of spectacular society to its limits.

Debord noted that McLuhan had begun to recognise the negative effects of the emerging corporate and global media spectacle. In 1990, Debord even wrote that McLuhan was abandoned by disciples who were anxious to distance themselves from his gloom, in order to get jobs in precisely these bloated industries. For Debord, McLuhan, 'the spectacle's first apologist, who seemed to be the most convinced imbecile of the century, changed his mind when he finally discovered in 1976 that the pressure of the mass media leads to irrationality and that it was becoming urgent to modify their usage'.[10] At least Debord did McLuhan the service of noting his change of tone.

To flesh out the circumstances of McLuhan's improbable return, I should outline his decline in order to assess the defects in his work, prior to applying it to the new technological media.

Deleting McLuhan

The Canadian literature professor, Marshall McLuhan, who reluctantly turned his attention to the structures of advertising, television and the early electronic computer, had fallen out of favour by the late 1970s. One reason for this was his failure to combine his technological inquiry with a political one. He understood politics as simply a response to technology: democracy, for example, would break down – as would the electorate – in the decentralised instantaneity of electronic communication. His model of media did not accommodate the role of political activity. For example, his statement that Afro-American culture was primarily in tribal relationship to a mechanical world, and caught between literacy and new electric media, could not really become an operative message for the diverse ethno-politicisation of academic discourse and its recognition of pluralist society. Genosko suggests that: 'The "backward is really superior" thesis was nothing less than a policy of repression completely lacking a political economic analysis of American racism and an acknowledgement, in any specific – embodied or historically situated – way whatsoever, of the history of slavery and the systematic eradication of Native Americans . . .'[11] McLuhan's primitivist and evolutionist views would not sustain critical analysis within recent discourses of ethnicity and 'post-colonial' studies.

McLuhan's deterministic and monolithic account of media necessarily foregoes a detailed analysis of political dynamics that shape and exploit media in different ways. Nothing that McLuhan said could adequately articulate the relationship between media, power and commerce. Jonathan Miller accused him of an 'abdication of political intelligence'.[12] Even his disciple Arthur Kroker tempered his own enthusiasm when he realised that McLuhan had no theory to analyse or interpret the relationship between the economy and technology or between corporate power and information, and substituted for political consciousness a contemplative stance of apolitical objectivity.[13]

Benjamin DeMott, in an observation that predates more recent criticisms of postmodern discourse's abandonment of reality in favour of surfaces, said that McLuhanism will make us 'rise to the certainty that style and method are all, that the visible – Vietnam or wherever – is not in any sense there. And having done this we can take off absolutely, fly up from the non-world of consciousness into the broad sanctuaries of ecstacy and hope.'[14] He quotes McLuhan's optimism about the computer, the technology of which promises a 'Pentecostal condition of universal understanding and unity . . . a perpetuity of collective harmony and peace'. DeMott prefers the term 'McLuhanacy' to describe this impossible world.

The sense of McLuhan's failure was acute for other critics who, in Levinson's view, were ignorant of the impact of his thought. He took umbrage with Bliss's review, which claimed that, 'Once exalted as oracular, Marshall McLuhan's theories now seem laughably inadequate as an intellectual guide to our times.'[15]

By 1974 McLuhan had reiterated his message that media needed to be understood in terms of their radical effects, in order to wake their users from a 'self-induced subliminal trance'. Otherwise they would be 'slaves'.[16] However, this version of consciousness-raising is still phrased as a matter of the viewer becoming aware of the medium's means of circulating information and their impact on individual and society. But does this realisation amount to liberation? Once this transcendence is achieved, then what? Waking from a media-trance does not in itself dissolve the political economy of media.

European thought, which brought with it deconstructionism and poststructuralism, seemed further to seal McLuhan's work from current theory. As Genosko says, he had a derisive view of Derrida and French philosophy, even though French intellectuals had begun to respond to his own ideas. As we shall see, the lessons of deconstruction stand between McLuhan and his application to virtuality.

McLuhan's insights on television, radio and other technological extensions had certainly caught the imagination of the media and provoked debate in academia. McLuhan's declared intention was to place his culture under sustained observation in order to show how the future might reveal itself in the present. He insisted that he did not predict the future, but probed for its current effects. However, the relatively slow development in media technology meant that his ideas could not be applied in altered circumstances. They therefore exposed themselves to the allegation that they were *ex post facto*, revealing what was already there, while being incapable of being tested as theory on a new object. No other technology had arrived to reveal whether his observations and views might be valid in the context of a new media environment. The corollary is that McLuhan has been criticised for proposing a paradigm for media that was insightful conjecture at best and incoherent, generalised inquisition at worst.

McLuhan's popularity also declined because of his rather ambivalent relation with corporate industry and media. By the mid-1970s, McLuhan's fame had peaked, and through the rest of the decade his popularity and influence waned. He had over-exposed his work in the media and had become a 'personality' (even appearing in Woody Allen's *Annie Hall*, 1977).[17] His co-authored books were receiving few reviews, and a changing political climate sidelined him. People 'found that he was too opportunistic; they found that he was too easy to buy, he was too available on the speech-giving circuit, and somehow a bad aura collected around him . . .'.[18] As Robert Fulford adds, McLuhan set out to sell his ideas to business and governments for money, and 'in order to do that he had to be famous; he wanted to be famous'.[19]

McLuhan's declining health understandably hindered his work's influence. He had been ill for some time, having initially had surgery for a brain tumour in 1967. He suffered a major stroke in 1979 and, cruelly, the man who favoured an extempore form of address was reduced to the use of a few words at a time. The man's cherished oral medium ('speech is the extension of thought') had become severely impaired.

In 1980, the Center for Culture and Technology was closed by the University of Toronto, either because McLuhan could not run it or, in Marchand's view, because it lacked funds. 'McLuhan showed up one evening and wept because his old office was in shambles.'[20]

McLuhan died in his sleep on 31 December 1980, on the very eve of the decade that heralded the greatest media revolution since Gutenberg. He was not able to witness the mass commercialisation of the computer, in which the microprocessor, the silicon chip, Bill Gates, Apple, Netscape and the modem inaugurated the age of the PC, the Internet, the World Wide Web and Virtual Reality. Neither could he engage with the accompanying discourses of cyberpunk, posthuman and cyborg theory and the explosion of academic courses in digital media. However, McLuhan's ideas did not disappear for long, and a combination of hard work by his inner circle and the realisation that his explorations might actually be relevant to the virtual age ensured his resurrection, aligning the foremost explorer of media with the new, virtual 'extensions of man'.

McLuhan's Cultural Economy

You can be quite sure that if there are going to be McLuhanites, I am not going to be one of them. I know that anyone who learns anything will learn it slightly askew. I can imagine that having disciples would become a very great bother.[21]

Marshall McLuhan

Before looking in detail at McLuhan's ideas and the problems of applying them to current media, I will outline the character of his revival. How has his work been reconstituted for the new century?

An answer lies in academia and the reinstitutionalisation of McLuhanism by former colleagues and students in Canada. Levinson and other writers on McLuhan have sought to maintain his standing and insights, and are therefore justifiably capitalising on the new technologies in order to reassert McLuhan's status. They are also testament to the new McLuhanite cultural economy which has benefited from the resurgence of the University of Toronto's McLuhan Program in Culture and Technology, after the place was shut down rather too precipitately following his death in 1980. It was reinvented as a 'McLuhan Studies Room', and launched along with an *Understanding McLuhan* CD-ROM. A significant number of books and websites of interest have been written or edited by ex-students, relatives and other participants in his courses or projects.

McLuhan's 'rediscovery', as his son Eric describes it, is assisted by the re-circulation of his ideas by his admirers,[22] yet Neo-McLuhanism could not be introduced to the culture unless prevailing techno-environmental conditions were suitable. The technological advances in computing and communications have enabled his supporters working in fields such as media studies to conjoin his work with the information revolution.

This task is, superficially, a simple one of referring to the shift in the technological world since his death. For example,

McLuhan's son observes that the last twenty years have seen the arrival of new media. These include the personal computer, fax, video-conferencing, virtual reality and CD-ROMs. Further inventions have arrived, such as WAP (Wireless Application Protocol) phones and MP3 digital music.

However, technological change *per se* does not fully validate the reintroduction of McLuhanism as a tool for exploring new media and environments. The question of his relevance remains to be answered. The challenge is met using a number of strategies.

A spurious one is used by Eric McLuhan, who claims that nobody else is studying these new forms of media, and thus ignores the avalanche of academic and popular writing on these developments, some of which I discuss later.

Another is to flag up the critically reflective perspective of McLuhan's thought. For example, Moos emphasises the educational value of his message, claiming that he provides the means to develop an awareness of the social and other effects of media. This consciousness-raising amounts to a 'form of civil defense against media fallout', in which the central role of culture should elevate creative processes necessary for survival.[23] This accords with McLuhan's promotion of artistic activity as an early warning system for society (which I discuss towards the end of this essay). It also connects with his criticism of educational deficits within the school, college and university systems, which failed to take critical account of the structural importance of electronic media, particularly television. This perspective highlights the capacity of McLuhan's thought to accommodate itself to future circumstances, particularly in his later, salutary writings on the potentially catastrophic effects of media – which include lines such as 'World War III is a secret dimension inherent to our own technology'.[24] Of course, Moos applies this *aperçu* to 21st-century technology in a conditional manner, in order to suggest that McLuhan *would* have drawn significance from the origin of the Internet in military communications technology. He also forces McLuhan's more esoteric ideas about computers into a scenario which presents the remote danger that artificial computer intelligence (see below) could lead to a 'type of World Wide Web that downloads WW3'.[25] McLuhan's work is phrased as a kind of pre-emptive detection device which, with a bit of an upgrade, will permit us to approach new technology with our understanding and perceptions attuned to the environment. As McLuhan said in 1967: 'If we understand the revolutionary transformations caused by new media, we can anticipate and control them.'[26]

McLuhanism is therefore cast as an educational tool which, if properly used, can expose the mechanisms by which media exert their effects on humans.

The return of McLuhan, however, necessarily raises questions about the specific relevance of his work to today's information networks. The interim between the decline of his influence and his reintroduction has seen both radical technological transformations and an emerging body of theory and study of their effects. McLuhan, therefore, is playing 'catch-up' in many respects. In order to do this, McLuhanism must test its broad assumptions against these new technological and intellectual environments, before the detail of its thought can be applied to the problematic concept of 'virtuality'.

Testing McLuhanism: The Problem of Prediction

He never predicted the future, never tried to. 'I'll tackle the really tough one: the present. Let me see if I can predict the present.'[27]

Eric McLuhan

[A future medium like a kind of computerised ESP would process] *consciousness as the corporate content of the environment – and eventually maybe even* [lead to] *a small portable computer, about the size of a hearing aid, that would process of*

*[sic] private experience through the corporate experience, the
way dreams do now.*[28]

Marshall McLuhan, 1967

It is assumed that McLuhan ignored the future in favour of an
analysis of his present culture. He saw his role as dissecting the
latter in order to supply humanity with the means to institute a
heightened awareness of advances in technology. This had its
historical dimension, because he strove to understand the television age in relation to long-term historical shifts and geo-
graphical differences in media and technology. His books had
outlined the development and effects of transitions from speech,
through alphabet and print, to electric media such as telegraphy
and radio, in order to illuminate the cultural environment of his
time.

Indeed, rather than phrasing the present in relation to the
future, he emphatically argued that the present was an effect of
the past. This is McLuhan's 'rear-view mirror' version of the
media, which are initially understood and conceptualised in
terms of previous technologies. 'When faced with a totally new
situation', he explains, 'we tend always to attach ourselves to
the objects, to the flavor of the most recent past. We look at the
present through a rear-view mirror. We march backwards into
the future.'[29] A typical example is the use by television of the
previous content of film, or the employment by the car ('horse-
less carriage') of the visual language of a previous medium of
transport. Computers use the technology of the typewriter and
the contents of television, telephone, fax, newspaper, etc.

In other words, McLuhan attempted to provide theories
based on historical evidence. However, while he sought to provide tools for understanding media that could be applied to
future circumstances, he was reluctant to adopt the role of
futurologist.

In terms of technological advances in media, this stance
makes McLuhanism vulnerable to accusations that its power is

blunted by its reluctance to get involved with detailed research on the political economy of media and its effect on media technology. His thought tends to suffer from a form of theoretical inertia, which renders his broad thesis too inflexible to account for the flux in the structural dynamics in media and communication.

For example, Castells claims that diversification of media (such as cable, digital and terrestrial TV) has led to a more extensive targeting of audiences according to lifestyles, and encountered a new dynamic of communication. This diversification and nicheing places McLuhanism under some duress. Castells argues that: 'While the audience received more and more diverse raw material from which to construct each person's image of the universe, the McLuhan Galaxy was a world of one-way communication, not of interaction . . . it fell short, McLuhan's genius notwithstanding, of expressing the culture in the information age. This is because processing goes far beyond one-way communication.'[30]

Castells contends that the first-generation utopian, communitarian and libertarian culture of users constructed the Net in two opposite directions. One was based on the restricted access to computer hobbyists with their pioneering spirit and distrust of commercialisation. The other was populated by 'newbies', for whom counter-cultural ideology still retains its informality and who subscribe to the principle that 'many communicate with many', and yet each person has a 'voice'. However, these newbies will reflect commercial interests because they will extend the power of major public and private organisations into the realm of communication. Castells therefore concludes that while this group has its commercial dimension, it is still situated in the culture of individuality: 'Unlike the mass media of the McLuhan Galaxy, they have technologically and culturally embedded properties of interactivity and individualization.'[31]

In this context, even McLuhan's dictum, 'the medium is the message', is obsolete. For Castells, the message is the medium:

the characteristics of the message shape the medium. For example, the medium of MTV is tailored in its entirety to its targeted youth audience.

At a more banal level, and despite McLuhan's claims to avoid prediction, his assumptions about technology also demand some considerable upgrading of his key ideas. In our age of networked computers, it is on face value prescient of McLuhan to use terms which are now familiar to us: 'The computer can be used to direct a network of global thermostats to pattern life in ways that will optimize human awareness. Already, it's technologically feasible to employ the computer to program societies in beneficial ways.'[32] Elsewhere he states that: 'You could run the world's biggest factory in a kitchen by a computer. With telephones, telexes, and computers – all of which operate at instant speeds – management and all forms of hardware can be centralized. The computer, literally, could run the world from a cottage.'[33]

McLuhan's observations reveal the limits of his thought, not only in relation to future technology but also in relation to the conclusions he drew from the media environment around him. His statement that electric technology leads to global instantaneity and decentralisation does not accord with his assumption that the technology of media still performs in centralist terms, whereby the world can be run from a localised database. His 1969 interview in *Playboy* demonstrates that his depiction of media as a homogeneous, one-way form of communication intrudes on his view of the computer. In the tradition of early science-fiction film, he suggests that the computer will become capable of programming media to 'determine the given messages a people should hear in terms of their over-all needs, creating a total media experience absorbed and patterned by all the senses'. Thus, McLuhan trades on a social-engineering view of computer technology, in line with the logic of the advertising industry. The mainframe will be capable of 'programming five hours less of TV in Italy to promote the reading of newspapers during an election', or provide a further 25 hours of TV in Venezuela to 'cool down the tribal temperature raised by radio the preceding month'. This ambitious prognosis is matched by McLuhan's fanciful idea that computers might be directly linked with private and collective consciousness and be able to process and communicate pure thought between the minds of individuals. These visions allow us to discern how the techno-romanticism of his time jars with the emerging techno-realism of our own, and blunts his predictive potential.

McLuhanism needs to be aligned with the dynamics of current computer-mediated communication, and attempts have been made to do just that. However, to explore this connection, we must first present the theoretical framework to which his ideas are being re-introduced, in order to inquire whether subsequent theoretical disciplines constitute obstacles to his new reception.

A Proto-Postmodernist? Theory Since McLuhan

A problem arises in the confrontation between McLuhan's model of media and subsequent theories and methodologies.

The issue, therefore, of McLuhan's relevance to our current situation must deal not just with technological advances in media, but also with discourses that have grown up around it, particularly the theories of 'virtuality' that have arisen since his death. In other words, McLuhanism must engage with theories that it either chose to sideline in its heyday or must now overcome in order to be viable.

A new development in the extensions of social communication had appeared which could put McLuhan's key ideas to the test, most notably Baudrillard's work on simulation. As Gary Genosko states, however, they had different agendas. Genosko argues that important theorists such as Paul Virilio and Jean Baudrillard extend and often implicitly criticise McLuhan's thought. Jean Baudrillard has been termed 'the French McLuhan', and his work in some respects bears superficial resemblances to the Canadian's views of media.[34] However, in the writing of both Baudrillard and Virilio a note of pessimism, if not cynicism, has replaced the positive tone that McLuhan set in the 1960s. For example, Virilio states that, 'At the end of the century, there will not be much left of the expanse of a planet that is not only polluted but also shrunk, reduced to nothing, by the teletechnologies of general interactivity.'[35]

In respect of the foundations of postmodern thought, McLuhan's early work has been compared with that of other writers on popular culture, including Roland Barthes and structuralists such as Lévi-Strauss, who attend primarily to the structure of the medium (i.e. language) rather than its content. Inherent to these claims is the notion that McLuhan is a prototypical postmodernist whose explorations of media anticipate the postmodern perspective that is marked by its emphasis on social fragmentation, pluralism and the full emergence of a consumer culture dominated by simulations, or signs detached from referents.[36]

McLuhan's texts and conception of language arguably prefigure postmodern theories of the writer, reader and textuality. For some, McLuhan's style prefigures the virtual world and outdates its own medium. His books are often paratactic in style – meaning that they are constructed from a disconnected set of propositions. In some cases they use graphic and photographic means to disrupt the reader's assumptions about the linearity or 'logic' of reason, while providing a visual 'hit' that corresponds to the total, non-hierarchical text of newspapers rather than the expository 'ABD and E'ness' of a linear text. The relative novelty of his style ensured that it was occasionally criticised for its elliptical, non-sequential, non-academic structure.

In the light of new technologies, this version of writing is revealed as a prescient form that wanted to escape the confines of linear literature. For example, Levinson argues that some of

McLuhan's books, such as *The Medium is the Massage* [*sic*], pre-dated the hypertext of the Web (e.g. the links on home pages) because they were constructed from a 'mosaic' set of fragments of text and image that could effectively be read in any order and in any direction according to the desires of the reader. It should be remembered that McLuhan was exploiting literary forms of montage and collage that are modernist in character, and his discussions do not stray far from references to typical examples such as James Joyce and Wyndham Lewis. Thus his relation to postmodernism must be qualified by the strong attraction he had for stylistic devices originating in early 20th-century literature.

The difference between McLuhan's work and high post-modern style and theory is not restricted to the issue of McLuhan's modernist references. It also extends to the philo-sophical assumptions on which his thought operates.

Postmodern culture is often broadly defined and debated as a triumph of image over reality, surface over depth, style over content and signifier over signified (or referent). In this para-digm, the primacy of a text's meaning and possible interpreta-tion is construed as an effect of a constant *semiurgy*: the mobil-isation and reconfiguration of signs in endless combination with multiple effects. Postmodernism therefore focuses attention on language and its multiplicity of codes. The extreme post-structuralist position argues that the world *is* a text, and that reality is a discursive construct. This textualisation of the world has an impact on McLuhanism, as I shall briefly show. It is characterised in part by the work of Jacques Derrida, whose deconstructive strategy asks us to consider whether McLuhan's historical assumptions about the primacy of speech over print and television may be misplaced.

To demonstrate this, Derrida reveals the subordinate posi-tion that the text previously occupied in history to speech and the spoken word. It is in this context that Derrida's thought poses a 'deconstructive' question to McLuhan. Does McLuhan consider the relationship between *text* and *speech* in his own writing? Seemingly not, since McLuhan presupposes that speech (oral/acoustic culture) must precede writing (visual/linear culture).

We can illustrate this decisive contention between McLuhan and Derrida by comparing the opposed use they make of Plato's distrust of writing. McLuhan quotes the famous passage in Plato's *Phaedrus* in which the invention of writing is condemned:

'. . . *this discovery of yours will create forgetfulness in the learners' souls, because they will not use their memories; they will trust to the external written characters and not remember themselves.*'[37]

This supports McLuhan's version of events, because 'until literacy deprives language of [t]his multi-dimensional resonance, every word is a poetic world unto itself'.[38] Thus, in line with Plato, McLuhan privileges speech/word over text/alphabet.

We can now consider Derrida's reading of the same passage in Plato. A completely different position results from Derrida's deconstructive criticism of Plato's negative verdict on writing, and, in particular, the function of *metaphor* (the description of one thing by another) in language. Plato sees writing as poisonous to the primacy and full *presence* of speech. Metaphors draw philosophy away from the immediacy of speech, because they are inherently *at a distance* from what they describe. Derrida deftly signals that in fact Plato himself is exploiting metaphor – for example, writing as a 'poison' – in order to secure the desired presence of speech.[39] Plato's defence of speech attacks writing as harmful, and, at the same time, represses the fact that it relies on writing.

McLuhan's work can therefore be deconstructed in a similar manner to reveal that his triphasic model of evolution in media (speech, writing/print, electronic media) is based on the metaphysics of the presence or immediacy of speech and the relegation of writing to a subordinate position. Genosko has come to McLuhan's rescue, against Derrida's criticism. McLuhan's vision of the end of the book (writing/print), in Genosko's view, announces the beginning of television, which has an 'aurality' and tactility irreducible to speech.[40]

Genosko's attempt to circumvent the challenge of deconstruction does not fully account for McLuhan's insistence on the primacy of 'speech' presence. Arguably, in McLuhan's paradigm, even the medium of television relies on this same metaphysical ghost of presence. Indeed, to go further, we could say with Derrida that the virtual reality environment is itself crucially dependent on maintaining presence and the immediacy of speech (the virtual discourse insists on the claim that 'you are *really* there').

McLuhan's place in the postmodern constellation is therefore a contradictory one, in which his subject-matter appears to chime with more recent theories of culture that emphasise technological factors. While McLuhan trades in the themes that, superficially, define postmodernism (e.g. the medium replacing the meaning), his model is constructed on a search for origins and a transparency of communication – assumptions that postmodern theory attempts to debunk. His thought is locked into a mode that could not be identified by McLuhan unless he had absorbed the lessons of deconstruction. It is therefore simplistic to describe him as a postmodernist *avant la lettre*.

With these caveats in place, we can approach the central issue of this book: McLuhan's encounter with 'virtuality'. The first task is to define this term, or rather demonstrate the polysemic and contested character of this discourse.

Understanding Virtuality – Links Between McLuhan and Narratives of New Media

If we let slip a yawn at the mere mention of virtual reality, cyberspace, and embodied virtuality, or roll our eyes at the naming of

*telepresence, teletopia, and electronic cloning, it is because
something has been missed in the headlong rush to exit the
common-or-garden experience of everyday life for the apparent
wonderment of the latest technologies.*[41]

New technologies and media have not only been accompanied
by discourses of virtuality, but have been constructed by them.
They all have a bearing on the assumptions that accompany
McLuhanism. The current discourse of virtuality springs from
science, literature, philosophy and socio-cultural studies. The
arrival of the computer has been presaged, dissected and
debated by theory and literature, including science fiction.
Cyberpunk, for example, is a genre that arose in the mid-1980s.
It often represents a dystopian world of the near future that is
organised and controlled along corporate capitalist lines and
transformed by new technologies which alter the body, provide
new forms of media, and construct the new geography of 'cyberspace'.[42]

The word 'cyberspace' was coined by cyberpunk writer
William Gibson, yet it is not a definition confined to science fiction. Rather, it has become a literary narrative that has affected
'the way that virtual reality and cyberspace researchers are
structuring their research agenda'.[43] The vision of cyberspace
that Gibson offers dovetails with dominant versions of postmodern thought. For example, Fredric Jameson, David Harvey
and Manuel Castells discuss 'global spatial totality', 'time-space
compression', 'globalisation' and 'the space of flows'. Arguably,
these models are sometimes over-generalised, and often too
vague to provide analytical power.

However, these paradigms have recently come under more
critical scrutiny. A history of the language of virtuality has thus
grown out of a relatively uncritical and initially crude set of
assumptions and become more measured and reflective. I wish to
outline this development in order to show how certain narratives
are organised according to certain philosophical presuppositions.

These broad features of 'digital discourse' should allow us to introduce the new context of McLuhan's thought.

Michael Heim distinguishes between two approaches to the term 'virtual reality' introduced in 1984 by Jaron Lanier (the founder of VPL – Visual Programming Languages). Heim's typology is relevant because it demonstrates the current elasticity of the term, and also the extent to which culture confuses 'the artificial with the real, and the fabricated with the natural'.[44] Lanier patented the data-glove, the head-mounted display and the data-suit – with the purpose of integrating them into what in 1987 he called 'a reality-built-for-two' or 'RB2'.

The whole point of virtual reality (VR), according to Lanier, is 'to share imagination, to dwell in graphic and auditory worlds that are mutually expressive'.[45] For Heim, this constitutes the 'strong' technologically determined version of virtuality, where virtual reality is an emerging field of applied science. The strong meaning refers to a particular kind of technology rather than a consensual hallucination, simulated drug trip or illusion that the computer supplies us with. This version exhibits the typology of 'immersion', 'interaction' and information 'intensity'. The sense of immersion 'comes from devices that isolate the senses sufficiently to make a person feel transported to another place'.[46] 'Interaction' describes the computer's ability to change a virtual scene, in which the user is immersed, in synchronisation with the user's own movement and point-of-view. Information 'intensity' defines the degree to which the virtual world can offer users information about their environment. This can lead either to the VR characters displaying sentient behaviour (they behave like real entities) or to the experience of 'telepresence' – in other words, the extent to which a user feels present in a virtual environment. This could involve a link with another environment from a distance (e.g. controlling a real robot on Mars within a VR environment which sends a high degree of data from Mars, converted into a high intensity of information for the user).

'Virtual' has been applied not just to technology and not

simply to the experience of interacting with simulations that have some computerised component. It extends into the 'real' itself. Heim states that this is the 'weak' or loose definition of VR. Everything – from automated teller machines which fulfil the function of a bank teller in a virtual (an 'as if') mode, to phone sex, e-mail and supposed 'real-life' experiences such as window-shopping – has now been dubbed 'virtual'. From its technological specificity to its use as a description or connotation of a 'condition', the meaning of virtuality has haemorrhaged.

McLuhan, of course, had no knowledge of virtual technology, so his version of virtuality is a 'weak' one, in which the virtual reality is expressed as the (ontological and epistemological) condition of 'as if', rather than being descriptive of a specific technology. However, his comments on the computer and on technology can still be related to immersion, interaction and information intensity in the loose sense. These themes are condensed in his theory of 'hot' and 'cool' media.

McLuhan says: 'A hot medium is one that extends one sense in "high definition". High definition is the state of being well filled with data.'[47] For example, a photograph is high definition (a high intensity of information, in Heim's term), while a cartoon has a low level of information. Likewise, the telephone is low definition because the ear is given only a restricted amount of information compared to radio. The corollary of this is consonant with Heim's 'interactivity', because so little is given in a cool medium that much has to be filled in by the listener/viewer/user: 'Hot media are, therefore, low in participation, and cool media are high in participation or completion by the audience.'[48]

Finally, the notion of 'immersion' applies in general form to McLuhan's observation that 'Electric media transport us instantly wherever we choose. When we are on the phone we don't just disappear down a hole, Alice in Wonderland style – we are there and they are here.' When we are on the phone, on the air or presumably online, we are in a sense absent from ourselves and with the other. In a 1978 essay in *New York Magazine*, McLuhan said that 'the sender is sent. The disembodied user extends to all those who are recipients of electric information.'[49] The principles that Heim outlines are therefore present in McLuhan's work in a rather fragmentary and nascent form. This demonstrates the flexibility of the 'weak' definition of virtuality, and reveals the properties of virtuality inherent to all electric and electronic media.

There is an important philosophical dimension to discourses of virtuality that underpins the dynamics of immersion and interaction. The accession to virtuality is analogous to the pathway from the individual and imperfect world to the unified and idealised world of cyberspace.

The accompanying themes of perfection and completion necessarily invite philosophical critiques of the language of virtuality, and Coyne employs the term 'techno-romanticism' in order to provide a template to discern how romantic, idealist and empirical traditions co-ordinate virtual narratives. The virtual narrative is not simply a consequence or by-product of recent cyber-theory or cyberpunk analysis. It draws on philosophical systems of thought that have origins in classical philosophy. Coyne, for example, explores the techno-romanticism of information technology, and the rationalist and empirical traditions upon which techno-discourse draws. He suggests that the human condition emerged through the romantic and rationalist-empirical discourses, 'between unity and fragmentation, transcendence and order, the ineffable, and the presumption of language'.[50] These discourses develop claims that we can transcend the embodied reality of our world towards unity, using the force of information technology.

A cursory glance at these philosophical strands reveals the obvious relevance of thought to virtual narratives. Plato separated the world into the realm of our senses (where appearances and things can deceive) and the intelligible realm of ideas – ideal and unchanging forms and immutable Good. Plotinus (AD 205–270) later deployed Plato's doctrine to claim that the soul strives to escape the material body and embrace the unity of the ideal real. The link with virtuality is expressed in the mode whereby digital narratives have absorbed the idealism of this Neoplatonic concept of *ecstasis*: the release of the soul from the body. In some virtual narratives, the soul is replaced by the mind – 'the means of *ecstasis* is immersion in an electronic data stream, and the realm of unity is cyberspace'.[51] This idealism is echoed by romantic idealist philosophers for whom the analytical, categorising, measuring powers of rationalism and empiricism distract the individual into studying particulars and conceal the perfection of unity. For Coyne, empiricism's emphasis on representation of space – its reduction and division – still leads to techno-romanticism: 'If computers allow us to model, mimic, and represent reality, then they indeed allow us to alter perceptual fields, challenge and distort reality, and create alternative realities. So rather than countering romanticism, empiricism provides the conditions for technoromantic narratives to promote the transcendent potential of computer space.'[52] McLuhan's version of technological humanism can be considered within this techno-romantic dimension:

By surpassing writing, we have regained our sensorial WHOLENESS, not on a national or cultural plane, but on a cosmic plane. We have evoked a super-civilized sub-primitive man.[53]

This statement also indicates that McLuhan's narrative of technology and media is not just premised on the romantic theme of unification or transcendence, but also includes a crucial element that is not normally present in virtual discourses. It distinguishes McLuhan's work from the pervasive and fashionable themes of posthumanism and simulationism, for his unique perspective is premised on a 'myth of return', via technology, to a pre-literate social reality. He sets up electronic (and presumably virtual) technology's destiny as the ability to turn society into a unified collective. 'We now live in a *global* village', he announces, 'a simultaneous happening. We are back in acoustic space. We have begun again to structure the primordial feeling, the tribal emotions (from which a few centuries of literacy divorced us) of a culture that preceded the invention of writing and printing.'[54]

At this time in history, according to McLuhan, the senses of 'man' were in harmony and completeness, and thus man was at one with himself and his environment. The role of speech and listening was central, and thus these societies lived in what he called an 'acoustic' world, in which communication involved highly interactive exchanges in which thought and action were inseparable. This culture was tribal, engaged, practical and unitary. When literacy arrived, the relationship between man and environment was changed by the new medium. Writing emphasised the visual rather than the oral and acoustic: 'A goose quill put an end to talk, abolished mystery, gave us enclosed space and towns, brought roads and armies and bureaucracies.'[55] It enabled us to lay out our thoughts in linear order and to conquer space by transporting them on paper. The mechanisation of printing – McLuhan's Gutenberg Galaxy – turned history into classified data, and the transportable book brought the 'world of the dead into the space of the gentleman's library'. But print also isolated the reader and silenced her voice and discussion. Telegraph brought the entire world to the workman's breakfast table. Electronic media brings us unification, in a techno-romantic fashion. McLuhanism claims ours is a brand-new world of 'all-atonceness' in which 'Time has ceased, "space" has vanished'.[56]

Unity, return and harmony are achieved by technological means, yet it is important to note the foundational concept on which McLuhan builds his technological humanism. It is the principle of sensory harmony, in which all senses have the potential of working in equitable relationship with one another when the capacity of media is optimised. When media deliver the requisite means to enable senses to work in accord, communication becomes inherently transparent, direct, full and immediate.

McLuhan's narrative presents electric technology as the apogee of this principle, because it facilitates all the conditions that are required for sensory harmony, transparency and immediacy.

McLuhanism is predicated on foundational humanist assumptions that aspects of postmodernism will seek to refute in terms of deconstruction. This is the issue at stake, despite McLuhan's application to obvious postmodern issues of globalisation, information and society. One key postmodern concern is with theories of language and representation in their relation to reality, whichever way it is defined. In a postmodern world, reality is sometimes alleged to have receded or been replaced by 'hyper-reality', a universe of images and codes that produce the real in their own terms. Language is constitutive of reality. The condition of virtuality is one that presupposes the same binary relationship between the virtual image (or medium) and reality. In postmodern terms, the primacy of the image over reality connects with the virtual narrative which contends that virtuality has affected reality in some way. Heim therefore argues that cyberspace is a tool for examining our sense of reality. However, this may take not only the examination of reality as itself a given, but also assume too much about the relation of the virtual to the real. A brief description of the significant versions of the relationship between virtual and real is necessary, if we are to place McLuhan within virtual discourse.

The articulation of virtuality with reality has several complexions, each of which attaches certain relative values to each term.

The first model constructs virtual reality as a 'false approximation' of reality (a degraded copy, simulation or too perfect a version of it); the second claims that it is a 'resolution' or 'hyper-realisation' of the real.[57] These positions are noticeable in narratives which assume that the immersion by the user in a virtual system is concomitant with a removal from the fullness and instability of real existence. For example, N. Katherine Hayles says: 'As we rush to explore the new vistas that cyberspace has made available for colonization, let us remember the fragility of a material world that cannot be replaced.'[58] The second version assumes that reality seems impoverished and that virtuality can complete it, rather like glasses can 'resolve' poor eyesight. Reality has within itself the possibility of its supplement *and* completion in virtuality (called 'suppletion' of the real).[59] Thus, different versions of the real and virtual are presented. A third, more extreme version depicts virtual reality as a total resolution of the real, in which humans could escape from the world and into technology (as in Moravec's downloading of consciousness into computers):[60] we would be obliged by scientists 'to step out of the world without leaving a trace. We would never have been (t)here.'[61]

A further dimension to these views is outlined in Heim's analyses of the function of realism and idealism in virtual narratives, which he performs in order to construct a more pragmatic approach ('virtual realism') to the issue of virtuality than that achieved by utopian and dystopian writings on cyberspace from the 1980s. He argues that: '[T]he network idealist builds collective bee-hives. The idealist sees the next century as an enormous communitarian buzz. The free circulation of information runs through the "planetary nervous system".' Heim comments that for the network idealist, 'The prospect seems so exciting that you see the phrase "virtual communities" mentioned in the same breath with McLuhan's "global village" or Teilhard's[62] "Omega Point".'[63]

McLuhan's view of a global community is often taken only in its positive, idealised state. However, Heim and others should be cognisant of McLuhan's qualifications to his thesis. McLuhan claims that: 'The global-village conditions being forged by the electric technology stimulate more discontinuity and diversity and division than the old mechanical, standardized society; in fact, the global village makes maximum disagreement and creative dialog inevitable.'[64] Problems of discourses on tribalism aside, the issue of the destructive effects of mass media and virtuality are often ignored in assessments of McLuhan's work. There is a danger of overemphasising the unitary, transparent and non-dialectical aspects of his thesis on the global village. Contradiction and conflict do exist in this equation.

The other side of the idealist coin is what Heim calls 'naïve realism'. This view of virtuality is one that defines virtual reality as a suppression of reality, to the point where computer systems are seen as alien intruders, where new media 'infiltrate and distort non-mediated experience until immediate experience is compromised'.[65] Attendant on this theme is the fear of losing local identity, interdependence and community as we merge in a virtual and global network. Naïve realism is not applicable to McLuhan's techno-idealism.

Finally, the fourth, radical and particularly postmodern account of virtuality contends that there is no distinction between virtuality and reality. This is because the real has always been virtual, as it is never fully present or actual. In other words, reality never intersects with itself, as it is constructed (like our identities) through difference and not presence. Language is the most obvious tool that separates us from ourselves while defining us to ourselves. This particularly 'weak' or loose definition of virtuality makes sense when the real is construed as socially and culturally constructed. For example, sociological method shows that our lives are always constructed through mediations and interactions.[66]

This dimension is paralleled in another form by psychoanalytic linguistic readings of reality and virtuality, or in the Lacanian trinity of the real, imaginary and symbolic. According to Žižek, if virtual reality is all surface, with no actual access to substance and the real, then we find this is also the case in real life outside virtual reality. Like VR, the real is surface, and it does not permit access to the 'true real'. Žižek notes that virtual reality shows us the virtualisation of the true reality: '[B]y the mirage of "virtual reality", the "true" reality itself is posited as a semblance of itself, as a pure symbolic edifice. That fact that "a computer doesn't think" means that the price for our access to "reality" is that *something must remain unthought*.'[67] For Coyne, this means that the ambitions of VR remind us that the real resists representation. In a romantic and sublime register, 'it is ineffable'.[68]

As we have seen, McLuhanism thrives on a triple narrative of initial unity (in primitive, oral cultures), fragmentation (in writing and print) and reunification (in electronic media). It provides an historical and spatial dimension, in which the proximity of 'man' to reality is contingent upon the technologies of media at each period in history or in each global location. Superficially, this might lead one to suppose that, for McLuhan, the relation between media and reality is conditional upon historical circumstances. However, McLuhan bases his analyses on a residual and ahistorical psychology of perception, wherein language/media/technology are oriented at all times towards the ratios between human senses – 'media are artificial extensions of sensory existence'.[69] Furthermore, for McLuhan, the optimisation of these senses – the parity and harmonious unity of sight, touch, sound – is the desirable objective of media. The electronic media enable this 'allatonceness'. He assumes that this unification and instantaneity, which defines new technology, augurs a *return* to reality. His reality, then, is one that is primarily sociopsychological but technologically enabled. In this framework, sociality has historically been lost because media have not just extended human senses beyond their immediate and unified domain, but divided human senses and fragmented human identity. New electronic media now permit a return to this lost reality, although McLuhan warns that we must be careful to use them correctly, and be assiduous in discerning their effects. Thus, we return with a heightened critical awareness to a state of collective, tribal consciousness. The return to social reality is analogous to a pre-linguistic state, and McLuhan stipulates that 'the new media [e.g. television] are not bridges between man and nature: they are nature'.[70]

In the context of the four versions of virtual-real relations outlined above, McLuhanism therefore requires some analysis of the definition of reality that is presupposed in its discourse. McLuhan did not involve himself with contemporary postmodern and deconstructive approaches to the question of the construction of the binary of language/media/image and reality. He took for granted the narrative of technology and media as returning us to a contradictory state of an advanced primitivism, but did not question the assumptions that construed this social reality and its conditions. If we were to compare his presuppositions about the relationship between the media and reality with the discourses of the virtual-real, we might then describe McLuhan's project.

First, McLuhan would not see virtual reality as a false version of reality. As a medium – and thus an extension of man's sensory faculties – it could not be false in itself, for it is defined as a prosthetic or extension, in which such epistemological criteria are irrelevant. To define cyberspace as 'unreal' or inauthentic in comparison to reality is itself deceptive. Indeed, McLuhan did not provide a distinction between authentic and inauthentic, for media generate the perception of change in the first place, and are not merely false representations of a coherent reality. The question of cyberspace's failure to live up to reality would instead have to be assessed according to the extent to which it orchestrated and mobilised man's senses as a unified sensorium. It would be found to fail 'reality' if it perpetuated the disequilibrium and fragmentation of the senses.

Second, the reverse contention that reality is impoverished and that virtual technology leads to its completion is only applicable to McLuhan's thesis if the historical narrative of his work is forgotten. In other words, McLuhan is adamant that at certain moments in history 'reality' was not impoverished. Tribal communities had a fully functional and integrated form of communication which electronic technologies would re-install.

Third, the assertion that virtuality will lead to a full-fledged escape from reality can only be considered in the context of McLuhan's religious and romantic claims of return and unification, and relative historical and technological conditions. His reality is defined as existing prior to the historical development of media since print, but emerging again under electronic media. In this sense, virtuality will mean a return to, and not an escape from, reality – even in the case of McLuhan's more extreme ideas of the computer's potential to enable the communication of pure thought without a medium (thus rendering the empirical reliance on the senses unnecessary).

Finally, McLuhanism is ambiguous on the postmodern 'reversal' in which reality is construed as a textual, symbolic and absent construction rather than the immediate existence and 'givenness' to experience that common sense and empiricism assume is foundational, even if open to debate. On the one hand, the phrase 'the medium is the message' seems to shift emphasis from the world that media purportedly represent and reorganise (the 'content'), to the operation of the codes by which such content is dispersed in the environment. On the other hand, McLuhanism is only superficially an aspect of postmodern logic. This is because the modern themes of anthropological and psychological origination and return (back to primitive, unified sensory states), and the primacy accorded to speech and presence over writing and absence (Derridean deconstruction), are in contradiction to the postmodern paradigm. This distinction is made clear by Coyne: 'Thus when critics of electronic media argue that the new symbolic environment does not represent "reality", they implicitly refer to an absurdly primitive notion of "uncoded" real experience that never existed.'[71]

McLuhanism's encounter with virtuality is therefore a problematic one, because it can be reduced to the themes of virtual discourse, yet it demonstrates a blindspot to the central strategies of postmodern thought. This lacuna in McLuhan's work is understandable, given the trajectory of his thought from modernist examples such as T. S. Eliot. Furthermore, while we can confer upon McLuhan's principles the gloss of postmodern theory, we have to consider that he was working within fairly restricted parameters.

Finally, the encounter of McLuhan with virtuality has been of the 'weak' variety. Postmodern theory claims that there is no separation between reality and symbolic constructions: the world is based on the production and consumption of signs. How, then, do we separate this general view of reality as virtual, from the 'strong' account of real virtuality? In contrast to earlier historical experience, what sort of communication system generates real virtuality? An answer is that it is a system in which reality itself (which is to assume rather too much about reality) is captured, and in which appearances are not mediated by the screen in our experience, but *become* that experience.

This inherent technological aspect of virtuality – the strong version of virtual reality – now needs comparison with the specific probes which McLuhan used.

McLuhan's Probes

The next medium, whatever it is – it may be the extension of consciousness – will include television as its content, not as its environment, and will transform television into an art form.[72]
Marshall McLuhan, 1967

Marshall McLuhan's explorations of media are now being reassessed for the virtual age. The primary theoretical assumptions of his work – the rear-view mirror, visual versus acoustic cultures, hot and cool media, and the tetradic theory of media (see Glossary) – can be applied to virtual technology and virtuality, and tested accordingly.

McLuhan claims that culture works like a rear-view mirror, because new media render previous ones obsolete while taking them as their content (e.g. the TV takes film as its material). Levinson supports this view, arguing that the digital environment absorbs the early mass-electronic environment while enhancing the global reach of the latter.[73] However, Levinson avoids falling into a simplistic view of McLuhanism, which relegates literate culture to a subordinate position in relation to the immediacy and 'wholeness' of oral culture. He does this by making salient both the superimposition and synthesis of written, visual and oral media within virtual cultures such as the World Wide Web, and the aspects of McLuhan's work that underline the hybrid character of media.

McLuhan defines the hybridisation of media as a 'civil war', in which 'the crossings or hybridizations of the media release great new force and energy as by fission or fusion'.[74] These dynamic exchanges are most turbulent when they can be expressed at a broad cultural level, in the confrontation between literate and oral cultures. At this macro-level, McLuhan tends to align these cultural conjunctions with debatable constructions of nationality and ethnicity. The Chinese, for example, release explosive energy on the arrival of literacy; conversely, the West is destabilised by the oral and tribal 'ear-culture' that the electronic media introduces to its formerly literate, individualised, text-based culture.

Levinson combines the hybrid model of media with McLuhan's principle that a medium has as its content a previous medium. With virtual technologies, the upshot is that the medium which serves as content for the Web is not one medium, but is composed of many media. It is a meta-medium. Levinson proposes that the Web has taken as its content 'the written word in forms ranging from love letters to newspapers, plus telephone, radio ("RealAudio" on the Web), and moving images with sound which can be considered a version of television'.[75] Virtual technologies, in the loose sense, are able to function 'as if' they were other media, because the computer – the technology that enables virtual culture – can absorb and emulate all other media. Indeed, given the amorphous and chameleon character of virtual media, there may be a case for jettisoning the term 'medium' altogether when considering the 'matrix' that includes the Web and Internet. Perhaps 'medium' is too loaded and isolationist a description in the virtual world.

Levinson is therefore claiming that the written word is not obsolete, but has become transfigured in the new medium. For him, the interactive medium, in which users in virtual space operate in immediate 'real-time' by using speech, writing and images, is the combination that 'conspired to make online communication a speech-like medium, a hybrid in which our fingers not only do the walking but the talking, from its inception'.[76] The two-way model of interaction supersedes McLuhan's historically restricted version of 'acoustic' media. He assumed that a tribal, immediate and connected culture could only be discerned within electronic media on account of the potential for satellite technology to connect people instantly with global events. In the virtual culture, the instantaneity of electronic messages and collective response is nothing compared to the realities of immediate intercommunication on e-mail, through e-conferencing and via WAP technology. Importantly, this virtual community turns consumers into *producers* of their own texts and images. Interaction involves pro-activity. The postmodern view of the reader-as-writer has an impact on McLuhan's view of media. It propels his version of the human subject, whose senses are involved to a greater or lesser degree with each medium (the cooler the medium, the more participation or filling-in by the senses of the viewer), to new heights.

The digital era has therefore problematised McLuhan's definitions of hot and cool media. In his world and method, television was a cool medium, which paradoxically stimulated participation on account of its low definition and lack of intensity, yet it prohibited any direct interaction, resulting in the frustration of viewers who wanted 'to reach out and touch someone, to get in touch'.[77] However, virtual technology, at least in its interactive setting, resolves this lack and fulfils the desire to participate. McLuhan acknowledged that the reader of texts could become an active participant in their construction (his montaged, 'mosaic' style was designed to exemplify this 'writerly' approach to texts). However, he could not have countenanced the extent to which the implosion of media consumption and production within the applications of the PC and computer would alter the definition of the user. In other words, despite his remarkable ability to draw our attention to the use of electronic media for linking users globally, he tended to underplay the extent to which users would actively participate in technology and media. His assumption about the degree of participation was framed by his emphasis on oral, tactile and acoustic involvement, in which a cool medium such as the telephone demands active involvement. However, this view of interaction presumes that users are participating *through* a medium, and that the degree to which they interact relies on the extent to which their senses (such as hearing) are involved. With virtuality, in its widest sense, the use of e-mail, e-conferencing and other tools demonstrates the shift from McLuhan's definition of the user as participant *through* a medium to manipulator *of* that medium. The telephone could not be manipulated as a medium; however, the computer is much more 'plastic' in its interactive possibilities. A typical computer monitor might have e-mail, Web chat, RealAudio, word-processing and a news ticker functioning at the same time. This would constitute a broad spectrum of hot and cool media on one screen, and the onus for their combination would fall on the hot and cool attitudes of the user, who is constructing a media environment for herself.

Despite this relative blind-spot, the possibility of shifting the emphasis of McLuhan's dictum 'the medium is the message' to a less well-known version of his project is therefore possible, because he also suggests that 'in all media the user is the content'.[78] Indeed, the term 'user' has replaced those of 'viewer' or 'audience' in Internet culture. The ideology of involvement cuts to the core of virtuality, and the user becomes the medium through which the Internet operates.

Levinson's revision of McLuhanism does not account for all virtual scenarios. It is certainly the case that, in virtual terms, print has become less visual and more acoustic, because it is now subject to the laws of oral culture. It can be used to communicate with another person or people directly, in real time, without the disadvantages of traditional print media. It can be combined with other media on the Internet, and it can undermine the linearity of the book by exploiting hyperlinks. The ability to click on highlighted words in a text on the Web places the onus on the user to construct that text while reading it, demolishing the primacy of the author and the integrity of the book. This holds true, in theory, for other media that the computer has absorbed.

There are virtual contexts that McLuhan could not have envisaged. For example, the narrative of totality, in which users become part of a collective, does not operate in situations where they are immersed in a virtual world that has no demonstrable application to the global village. Computer games, for example, can be played in isolation, where the only contact is between a user and a program that has been constructed and marketed by a corporate industry. Virtuality invites the immersion of the user in an environment that has nothing to do with participation. However, this narcissistic feedback loop is buckling under the 'urge to merge', because most popular games are now networked. They enable businesswomen in New York to adopt on-screen characters in *Quake II*, *Doom VII* and other corporate games, in order to wreak virtual and reciprocated carnage on individuals from Princeton to Poole. Thus, McLuhan's repeated warning that the non-critical fascination of users with their medium – the Narcissus narcosis – would blind society to the benefits and disadvantages of its media, becomes the logic of virtual immersion in these cases.

Perhaps the most significant application of McLuhan's ideas to virtuality lies in his work on the tetrad (see Glossary), which was published posthumously. The tetrad was the culmination of his attempt to formulate laws of media in order to provide a scientific basis to his explorations, and to condense his disparate insights into media in one neat set of questions. The application of the tetrad to virtuality arguably presumes that, first, a computer can be taken as representative of the virtual condition in general, and second, that it can be considered a medium in the same way as, say, television.

By applying McLuhan's four laws or effects of media, we can answer the following questions.

To the question of what aspects of society the new medium enhances or amplifies, we can answer that it increases the participation in the medium that was merely suggested in the relatively low definition of television, while at the same time promoting interactivity between participants at a global level. In response to the question of the aspects of media dominant before the arrival of the medium that it renders obsolete, we can suggest that it partially eclipses the telephone, the typewriter, the paintbrush, the paper fax and the CD, to name a few. In answer to the question of what the medium returns to prominence from previous obsolescence, we can reply that it reinvents the written letter in the form of e-mail. Lastly, we can answer the question of what the medium reverses or turns back into when it has run its course or been developed to its fullest potential as follows: it is already turning into the WAP (Wireless Application Protocol) mobile phone, which now carries websites and e-mail. These portable, palm-sized devices will soon be able to show Keanu Reeves films and provide live 'narrow-casts' of Manchester City's football matches. The computer will be miniaturised and absorbed in the digital watch, and it will become the content of digital television. Eventually the desktop computer will be perceived as a hindrance and a quaint, primitive artefact.

The question remains, however, of whether McLuhan's ideas

can transcend their own historical limitations, cast off their notions of global consciousness, 'dropping out', 'acting cool', *and* compete with prevailing and persuasive analyses of virtual culture. The effort to relate his probes to the present era of communications seems, in my view at least, hamstrung by a structural problem with his original work. This is its lack of engagement with the political economy of mass media, and its refusal to consider the content of media in any way other than as an irrelevance. There is no room in his thesis for analysis of the role of resistance to the message of the medium, and a cynic might argue that there is only a slim possibility that McLuhanism can survive without undergoing what amounts to a radical reorientation to socio-economic and political factors. A thorough critique of McLuhan's work would have to broach issues of multi-corporate global capital, access to new technologies, surveillance and censorship, monopolisation of software. Levinson has attempted to do this in his work on McLuhan, but the attempt to upgrade him in this context does seem restricted by the models that McLuhan prescribed.

This is not to say that the brave new world of virtual discourse is itself without its blunt edges. My final discussion addresses the dominant discourses on virtual identity and embodiment in relation to the work of McLuhan. Perhaps McLuhan can provide the means to temper more strident versions of cyborg theory.

Disincarnate Humans and Disconnected Identities

In the sense that these media are extensions of ourselves – of man – then my interest in them is utterly humanistic.[79]

Marshall McLuhan

McLuhan intersects with current debates on 'virtual identity' and the relationship of the body, identity and electronic technologies.

The discourse on virtual identity has three main inflections. Donna Haraway's cyborg theory, for example, underlines the narratives of suture, rupture and loss of bounded identity and their political potential. Her ground-breaking and provocative feminist manifesto for cyborgs proposes that such breaches of identity should be welcomed: the 'transgenic hybrids' that genetic engineering could create open up the possibility of a cybernetic, postfeminist libertarianism. The posthuman figure of the cyborg breaches the boundary between nature and artifice, body and machine. Haraway claims that this provides the entirely new alternatives of hybridisation to gendered identity being coded as 'natural' or 'artificial'.[80]

Conversely, Sherrie Turkle affirms that immersion in a networked computer can provide the user with a number of identities, so that the self becomes endlessly multiplied. While this actualisation of the self seems to echo Haraway's view, Turkle's construction of virtual identity does not lead towards radical disruption, contradiction and fragmentation, but to a condition in which the persona and the self converge. She points to the ability of the Internet to cultivate 'psychological well-being', and speaks of new identities as 'multiple yet coherent' in a permeable relation between the virtual and the real, 'each having the potential for enriching and expanding the other'.[81]

A third position draws attention to the relation of the body to new technology. N. Katherine Hayles asserts that, 'At the end of the twentieth century, it is evidently still necessary to insist on the obvious: we are embodied creatures.'[82] This formulation is intended to counteract virtual theories that place too much weight on the connection between consciousness and the computer. It reintroduces the body into the equation, and thus provides a caveat against discourses that conflate the real with the virtual, in which the mind is unproblematically represented as escaping from the body into cyberspace.

To some extent, this position also correlates with Heim's plea for a pragmatic and cautious approach ('virtual realism') to the subject of identity. Heim asks us to acknowledge a complex relationship with computers, and avoid 'glib exaggerations such as "Now we're cyborgs", or "Everything's virtual reality"'.[83] Of course, this assertion could lead one to suggest that perhaps Hayles's emphasis on embodiment is itself an exaggeration and a generalised abstraction of the role of the body in the virtual equation.

McLuhan's ideas can usefully be plotted according to these discourses on virtual identity. For example, the issue of embodiment and disembodiment in virtual identity is echoed in McLuhan's image of 'disincarnate man'. However, this figure is removed from the ego psychology of Turkle, for its disembodied character is registered within the 'anxious' discourse of virtuality. Here, any positive effects of the sensory shifts that television induces have resulted in the disincarnation of the viewer – a consequence of a psychic shock that the individual undergoes when exposed to media that weaken his or her sense of having a physical body and an autonomous identity. This is particularly burdensome for younger members of society, for McLuhan claims that, 'From Tokyo to Paris to Columbia, youth mindlessly acts out its identity question in the theater of the streets, searching not for goals but for roles, striving for an identity that eludes them.'[84]

McLuhan's version of disembodiment therefore cuts across superficial readings of the collectivism of the global village and the elevation of humans to a cosmic consciousness. For McLuhan, immersion in electronic media does not merely imply an elevation to a sublime state of global union, because his model incorporates the (admittedly under-theorised) conception that such immersion has a psychological and sensory impact that profoundly affects the ontological security of the individual. Presumably, virtual technology in its strict sense – virtuality as a condition – would exacerbate this threatening disincarnation or disembodiment: 'Mental breakdown of varying degrees is the very common result of uprooting and inundation with new information and endless patterns of information.'[85] Always the educationalist, McLuhan warns us that unless we are aware of this dynamic, we shall enter a phase of 'panic terrors, exactly befitting a small world of tribal drums, total interdependence, and superimposed co-existence'.[86]

Conclusion: Virtual McLuhan

McLuhan's message that we should be made aware of the media, and send out constant probes in order to test their effects, constructs an important role for a critically reflective approach to virtuality. This mantle is conferred upon specific members of society, particularly artists and writers. McLuhan, following Ezra Pound, had stated that artists perform the role of 'antennae', using perceptions that are attuned to shifts in media, and thus behave as early warning systems. They therefore reverse the 'rear-view mirror' scenario, providing navigational guides for the new (virtual) environment, rather than making the old environment their content. This is a modernist avant-garde position, and perhaps it is presumptuous of McLuhan to define art as a process through which sensory awareness expresses itself in its most acute form. However, McLuhan's overarching maxim – that an awareness of the medium as a message is to be considered ahead of its content – is intended to provide critical tools that will enable others to perform McLuhanite probes into virtual media. McLuhan expressed the view that there would be no McLuhanites, in the sense that his probes were for him alone. This leaves the ground open to others who wish to take up where he prematurely left off. It is understandable, therefore, that the McLuhan facility at the University of Toronto has introduced The Virtual Reality Artists' Access Program, providing a virtual space to explore critically artistic uses of interactivity and transinteractivity: the 'dialogue of bodies interacting in a virtual tactile space'.[87] Perhaps this is a robust response to McLuhan's urgent announcement that: 'The artist today might well inquire whether he has time to make a space to meet the spaces that he will meet.'[88]

The question of whether McLuhan's ideas themselves will be transfigured to illuminate virtuality and its discourses remains intriguing. The Canadian satellite of McLuhanism continues to beam his message to the world, but it can no longer trade on the force of his personality, the magnetism of his lecturing style and his omnipresence in the press and on television. When McLuhan died, his influence dissipated. Reviving it will require not only the virtual conferences, websites and embodied practices of virtual art, but also the critical acceptance of the value of his work in institutes and on courses beyond the localised McLuhanite environment of Toronto. It remains to be seen whether the new technologies will be able to disseminate his message as effectively as Marshall McLuhan did through his chosen media.

Notes

1. Paul Benedetti and Nancy DeHard (eds), *Forward Through the Rearview Mirror: Reflections on and by Marshall McLuhan* (Ontario: Prentice Hall Canada Inc., 1997), p. 171.

2. Marshall McLuhan and G.E. Stearn, 'Even Hercules had to Clean the Augean Stables but Once!: A Dialogue', in *McLuhan: Hot & Cool* (ed. G.E. Stearn) (Harmondsworth: Penguin, 1968), p. 302.

3. Marshall McLuhan, *Understanding Media: The Extensions of Man* (London: Ark, 1987), p. 7.

4. Paul Levinson, *Digital McLuhan: A Guide to the Information Millennium* (London: Routledge, 1999), p. 2.

5. Andrea Huyssen, 'In the Shadows of McLuhan: Jean Baudrillard's Theory of Simulation', *Assemblage* 10, pp. 7–17.

6. Gary Genosko, *McLuhan and Baudrillard: The Masters of Implosion* (London and New York: Routledge, 1999), p. 13.

7. Richard Coyne, *Technoromanticism: Digital narrative, Holism and the Romance of the Real* (Cambridge, Mass.: MIT, 1999), p. 304.

8. Ibid., p. 63. Coyne cites Wasson's claim that McLuhan reads the new technological environment as a 'book of symbols which reveals the Incarnation. Because everything in the world is a symbol, McLuhan can offer symbolic interpretation.' See R. Wasson, 'Marshall McLuhan and the Politics of Modernism', *Massachusetts Review* 13 (4), pp. 567–80. See also McLuhan, op. cit., 1987, p. 61.

9. Michel A. Moos (ed.), *Media Research: Technology, Art, Communication: Essays by Marshall McLuhan* (Amsterdam: G+B Arts International, 1997), p. xvi.

10. Guy Debord, *Comments on the Society of the Spectacle* (London: Verso, 1990), pp. 33–4.

11. Genosko, op. cit., p. 108.

12. Jonathan Miller, *Marshall McLuhan* (New York: Viking, 1971), p. 76.

13. Genosko, op. cit., p. 79.

14. Benjamin DeMott, 'Against McLuhan', in *McLuhan: Hot & Cool*, pp. 282–3.

15. Levinson, op. cit., p. 29.

16. Benedetti and DeHard, op. cit., 'Making Contact with Marshall McLuhan', interview by Louis Forsdale, 1974, p. 198.

17. While he queues to watch a film, Woody Allen's character chastises a media lecturer for loudly pontificating on McLuhan's ideas and mistaking television for a hot medium. Allen happens to have McLuhan at the scene. 'You know nothing of my work', says McLuhan to the academic. 'You mean my whole fallacy [*sic*] is wrong. How you ever got to teach a course in anything is totally amazing.'

18. Benedetti and DeHard, op. cit., 1997, p. 174.

19. Ibid.

20. Ibid.

21. Marshall McLuhan and G. E. Stearn, 'A Dialogue', in *McLuhan: Hot & Cool*, p. 335.

22. Benedetti and DeHard, op. cit., 1997, p. 183.

23. Moos, op. cit., 1997, p. 166.

24. Marshall McLuhan and Barrington Nevitt, *Take Today: The Executive as Dropout* (New York: Harcourt Brace Jovanovich, 1972), in Moos, op. cit., p. 165.

25. Moos, op. cit., p. 166.

26. Benedetti and DeHard, op. cit., 1997, p. 198.

27. Ibid., p. 186.

28. Eric McLuhan and Frank Zingrone (eds), *Essential McLuhan* (London: Routledge, 1997), p. 297.

29. Marshall McLuhan and Quentin Fiore, *The Medium is the Massage: An Inventory of Effects* (Harmondsworth: Penguin, 1967), pp. 74–5.

30. Manuel Castells, *The Information Age: Economy, Society and Culture; Volume I: The Rise of the Network Society* (Malden, Mass. and Oxford: Blackwell, 1996), p. 341.

31. Ibid., p. 358.

32. *Playboy* interview (1969), 'Marshall McLuhan – A Candid Conversation with the High Priest of Popcult and Metaphysician of Media', in E. McLuhan and Zingrone, op. cit., p. 263.

33. Benedetti and DeHard, op. cit., p. 177.

34. See Jean Baudrillard, *In the Shadow of the Silent Majorities* (New York: Semiotext(e), 1983), and *The Ecstasy of Communication* (New York: Semiotext(e), 1987).

35. Paul Virilio, *Open Sky* (London: Verso, 1997), p. 21.

36. David Harvey, *The Condition of Postmodernity: An Enquiry into the Origins of Cultural Change* (Oxford and Cambridge, Mass.: Basil Blackwell, 1989), p. 289.

37. Marshall McLuhan, *The Gutenberg Galaxy* (London: Routledge and Kegan Paul, 1962), p. 25.

38. Ibid.

39. Jacques Derrida, 'Plato's Pharmacy', in *Dissemination* (London: Athlone Press, 1981), pp. 61–171.

40. Genosko, op. cit., pp. 41–2.

41. Marcus A. Doel and David B. Clarke, 'Virtual Worlds: Simulation, Suppletion, S(ed)uction and Simulacra', in Mike Crang, Phil Crang and John May (eds), *Virtual Geographies: Bodies, Space and Relations* (London and New York: Routledge, 1999), p. 261.

42. James Kneale, 'The Virtual Realities of Technology and Fiction: Reading William Gibson's Cyberspace', in Crang, Crang and May (eds), op. cit., p. 29.

43. David Tomas, 'Old Rituals for a New Space: Rites of Passage and William Gibson's Cultural Model of Cyberspace', in M. Benedikt (ed.), *Cyberspace: First Steps* (Cambridge, Mass.: MIT Press, 1991), p. 46.

44. Michael Heim, *Virtual Realism* (Oxford and New York: Oxford University Press, 1998), p. 4.

45. Ibid., p. 16.

46. Ibid., pp. 6–7.

47. McLuhan, op. cit., 1987, p. 22.

48. Ibid., p. 23.

49. Levinson, op. cit., p. 39.

50. Coyne, op. cit., p. 7.

51. Ibid., p. 10.

52. Ibid., p. 106.

53. Marshall McLuhan, *Counter-blast* (London: Rapp and Whiting, 1970), p. 16.

54. McLuhan and Fiore, op. cit., p. 63.

55. Ibid., pp. 14–16.

56. Ibid., p. 63.

57. Doel and Clarke, op. cit., p. 261.

58. N. Katherine Hayles, *How We Became Posthuman: Virtual Bodies in Cybernetics, Literature, and Informatics* (Chicago and London: University of Chicago Press, 1999), p. 49.

59. Doel and Clarke, op. cit., p. 268.

60. Hans Moravec, *Mind Children: The Future of Robot and Human Intelligence* (Cambridge, Mass.: Harvard University Press, 1988).

61. Doel and Clarke, op. cit., p. 277.

62. Pierre Teilhard de Chardin was a Jesuit palaeontologist who predicted the unification of human consciousness and spirit in a single, enormous 'noosphere' or 'mind sphere'. The noosphere network would embrace the earth, marshalling planetary resources in a world unified by love. This echoes Hegel's philosophy of the birth of Spirit as the immanent purpose of historical change. See Pierre Teilhard de Chardin, *Phenomenon of Man*, trans. Bernard Wall (New York: Harper, 1959).

63. Heim, op. cit., p. 39.

64. E. McLuhan and Zingrone, op. cit., p. 259.

65. Heim, op. cit., p. 37.

66. See Peter L. Berger and Thomas Luckmann, *The Social Construction of Reality: A Treatise in the Sociology of Knowledge* (London, New York, Victoria, Toronto and Auckland: Penguin, 1991).

67. Slavoj Žižek, *Tarrying with the Negative: Kant, Hegel, and the Critique of Ideology* (Durham, N.C.: Duke University Press, 1994), p. 44.

68. Coyne, op. cit., p. 269.

69. McLuhan, op. cit., 1970, p. 116.

70. Marshall McLuhan, *Verbi-Voco-Visual Explorations* (New York, Frankfurt and Villefranche-sur-Mer: Something Else Press, Inc., 1967a), unpaginated.

71. Coyne, op. cit., p. 373.

72. E. McLuhan and Zingrone, op. cit., p. 296.

73. Levinson, op. cit., p. 18.

74. McLuhan, op. cit., 1987, p. 48.

75. Levinson, op. cit., pp. 37–8.

76. Ibid., p. 33.

77. Ibid., p. 112.

78. E. McLuhan and Zingrone, op. cit., p. 276.

79. McLuhan and Stearn, op. cit., p. 329.

80. Donna Haraway, 'A Cyborg Manifesto: Science, Technology and Socialist-Feminism in the 1980s', in *Simians, Cyborgs, and Women* (London: Routledge, 1989).

81. Sherrie Turkle, *Life on the Screen: Identity in the Age of the Internet* (London: Weidenfeld and Nicolson, 1995), p. 268.

82. N. Katherine Hayles, 'Embodied Virtuality', in *Immersed in Technology: Art and Virtual Environments*, Mary Anne Moser (ed.)

with Douglas MacLeod (Cambridge, Mass. and London: MIT Press, 1996), p. 3.

83. Heim, op. cit., p. 47.

84. E. McLuhan and Zingrone, op. cit., p. 249.

85. McLuhan, op. cit., 1987, p. 16.

86. Marshall McLuhan, *The Gutenberg Galaxy* (London: Routledge and Kegan Paul, 1962), p. 32.

87. Genosko, op. cit., p. 11.

88. Marshall McLuhan and Harley Parker, *Through the Vanishing Point: Space in Poetry and Painting* (New York, Evanston and London: Harper Colophon Books, 1969), p. 31.

Select Bibliography

Paul Benedetti and Nancy DeHard (eds), *Forward Through the Rearview Mirror: Reflections on and by Marshall McLuhan*, Ontario: Prentice Hall Canada Inc., 1997.

Paul Levinson, *Digital McLuhan: A Guide to the Information Millennium*, London: Routledge, 1999.

Gary Genosko, *McLuhan and Baudrillard: The Masters of Implosion*, London and New York: Routledge, 1999.

Philip Marchand, *Marshall McLuhan: The Medium and the Messenger*, New York: Ticknor and Fields, 1989.

Marshall McLuhan, *Understanding Media: The Extensions of Man*, Cambridge, Mass. and London: MIT Press, 1994.

Eric McLuhan and Frank Zingrone (eds), *Essential McLuhan*, London: Routledge, 1997.

Websites
http://www.mcluhan.utoronto.ca
http://www.ctheory.com

Glossary

The medium is the message

The human's use of any communications medium has an impact that is of more relevance than the content of any medium, or what that medium may convey. The process of being in a virtual environment, for example, has a greater effect on our existence than the program in which we are immersed. The act of watching television has had a greater impact than what is shown on the television.

The rear-view mirror

When society and the individual are confronted with a new situation, they will attach themselves to objects of the recent past. We therefore perceive the present through a rear-view mirror. New media, including the car and the computer, are initially looked at in terms of previous technologies, such as the horse-drawn carriage and the typewriter.

Visual and acoustic media environments

When information is simultaneous from all directions at once, the culture is auditory and tribal. Although these cultures may superficially appear to be attached to the ear and mouth, for McLuhan the crucial criterion is that the media environment in which individuals communicate must have simultaneity and instantaneity of communication. Thus, even apparently visually oriented media such as newspapers are in fact more aural in their presentation, because they provide a sense of information coming from everywhere in the world at once and being arranged in a non-linear fashion on the page. Virtual technology is thus an acoustic medium, for it has a high degree of tactility, immediacy and 'all-aroundness'. It is a medium of the 'ear' rather than the eye.

Visual cultures, on the other hand, substitute an eye for an ear. The eye has a point of view, which the ear does not. It internalises speech through writing, and separates individuals through print. It favours a linear, abstract format – commonly called text – and thus compels individuals to understand the world using a principle of 'one thing at a time'. The Western world has been dominated by the visual order, 'with procedures and spaces that are uniform, continuous and connected'.[1]

Hot and cool media

The basic principle that decides whether a medium is hot or cool is the degree to which that medium extends one sense in 'high definition'. In other words, it is the extent to which one of our senses is supplied with a lot of data. A photograph has more information than a cartoon, and is therefore a hotter medium. The telephone is a cool medium because the ear receives little information. The user therefore has more participation in a cool medium than a hot one.

The issue becomes more complicated with a 'meta-medium' such as the computer, in which a variety of hot and cool media (RealVideo and e-mail, for example) are superimposed and juxtaposed. In this context, virtual reality is arguably a very cool medium indeed.

Tetrad

This sets out McLuhan's four laws or effects of media: amplification, obsolescence, retrieval, reversal. What aspects of society does the new medium enhance or amplify? What aspects of media that were dominant before the arrival of the medium in question does it eclipse or render obsolescent? What does the medium return to prominence from previous obsolescence? And what does the medium reverse or turn back into when it has run its course or been developed to its fullest potential?

Note

1. Marshall McLuhan and Harley Parker, *Through the Vanishing Point: Space in Poetry and Painting* (New York, Evanston and London: Harper Colophon Books, 1969), p. 1.

Acknowledgements

Thanks to Toby Clark, Duncan Heath, Cristina Mateo, Ron Delves, Fran Lloyd, the staff and students in the Faculty of Design, Neal White, and De Geuzen Institute in Amsterdam.

Index